WELCOME TO SEX!

YOUR NO-SILLY-QUESTIONS GUIDE

First published in Great
Britain in 2024 by Gallery YA,
an imprint of Simon & Schuster UK Ltd

First published in Australia in 2023
by Hardie Grant Children's Publishing

1 3 5 7 9 10 8 6 4 2

Simon & Schuster UK Ltd
1st Floor, 222 Gray's Inn Road
London WC1X 8HB

Simon & Schuster:
Celebrating 100 Years of Publishing in 2024

www.simonandschuster.co.uk
www.simonandschuster.com.au
www.simonandschuster.co.in

Simon & Schuster Australia, Sydney
Simon & Schuster India, New Delhi

A CIP catalogue record for this book
is available from the British Library.

PB ISBN 978-1-3985-3320-2
eBook ISBN 978-1-3985-3322-6

Printed and Bound in Italy by L.E.G.O. S.p.A.

DR MELISSA KANG & YUMI STYNES

WELCOME TO SEX!

YOUR NO-SILLY-QUESTIONS GUIDE

ILLUSTRATED BY JENNY LATHAM

GALLERY YA
Simon & Schuster

start here

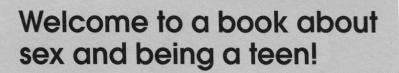

Welcome to a book about sex and being a teen!

Naturally, you're curious about sex.

Maybe you've noticed changes in the way your body reacts to touch, and it feels awesome! And maybe the **idea** of sex (which made you giggle or shout 'Gross!' when you were a kid) has suddenly started to seem like it could be ... OK? Or even great?

Managing these new sexy thoughts and feelings can be tricky, and the information available is sometimes unhelpful or wrong. It's like being on your L-plates, but without a straightforward set of instructions for how to actually drive! So we've crammed as much realness into this book as possible so that you've got a rock-solid resource on sex that you can trust.

'L-plates sex' is about doing as much safe learning as possible before you hit the road. It's about getting to know your own body first and what feels good. We have sections on what counts as sex, why people do it and what 'sexual identity' means.

There's a section on getting intimate with someone else, dating and hooking up. It's totally OK if you're not ready for any of that. By learning the basic principles of pleasure and consent, you'll be able to survive embarrassing moments, which may include a wobbly start, and opt into – or out of – sex, feeling fully informed and empowered.

We talk a lot about pleasure in this book because it's often **missing** from school sex ed, yet is one of the main reasons people have sex! Whatever your ability, gender, sexual orientation and identity, religion or culture, this book is really about how to feel good – in your body, in your mind, and about who you are.

The amazing thing is, you never really stop learning about sex. The learning happens in lots of ways over your whole life. This book is to help you understand the basics so that you get to know yourself first, and feel more confident, more in your power and more in control.

Have fun!

Dr Melissa and Yumi xx

For over 20 years, Dr Melissa answered questions from teens in an Australian magazine column called Dolly Doctor. Questions like: What IS sex? When will I have sex? Why do people have sex? Why do they not have sex? What is masturbation? How are you supposed to know when you're ready? What if you're not interested at all? Why is sex so confusing? And what actually happens when you 'do it'? In other words – A LOT OF QUESTIONS. We've shared some of these letters in this book so that you can see what other teens want to know. And, luckily, we can answer them all!

A NOTE ABOUT WORDS AND LABELS USED IN THIS BOOK

When we talk about sex and pleasure we're not just talking about body parts and feelings, but also about people and relationships. We'll use words like 'person', 'teen', 'penis-owner' or 'vulva/vagina-owner' a lot of the time. On occasion we might use 'girl/woman' or 'boy/man' when we're talking about cisgender people and referring to a specific question or story or research: for example, 'research shows that heterosexual women don't care that much about penis size'.

Contents

DO NOT DISTURB

WHAT IS SEX?

MORE ON p. 52

Sex is doing anything with your body that feels sexy. It can be 'solo sex' (known as masturbation). It can be touching another person's body with your hands or other parts of your body, rubbing genitals together, or kissing or touching breasts, nipples or parts of the body that turn you both on. Doing sexy stuff on the phone or online with another person is also sex. Sex might involve being totally naked, or partly or even fully clothed.

For many people, emotions are part of the definition of sex. Each person's definition of sex can change, depending on circumstances and timing. **The most useful definition of sex is 'what sex means to you'.**

Defining sex is beautifully complicated. Sex is anything as long as the people taking part in it think it is sex. It excludes violence, and it includes pleasure. *Professor Alan McKee*

8

We get that sex has different meanings in different cultures. You'd be excused for thinking 'penis-in-vagina sex' is the only 'real sex' there is – if you were basing it on movies, sex ed classes and religious teaching. Or for thinking that it's the only sex that matters. But it's not. Sex is SO much more diverse, fun and interesting! There's plenty of room in the world for us to value and respect all types of sex. And it's totally OK to be curious about all of it!

BTW: THESE DEFINITIONS OF 'SEX' ARE ABOUT DOING SEXY STUFF WITH OUR BODIES. THERE'S ANOTHER DEFINITION OF SEX THAT'S TO DO WITH PHYSICAL PARTS OF OUR BODIES, LIKE GENITALS, CHROMOSOMES AND HORMONES. THESE ARE ALSO CALLED SEX CHARACTERISTICS AND CAN LOOK A BIT DIFFERENT FOR EVERYONE, INCLUDING FOR PEOPLE WHO HAVE INTERSEX VARIATIONS (SEE PAGE 79).

The sexy 'feeling' can be thrilling, edgy, new, hot or tingly. It can feel a bit private. Often the sexy feelings can be all through your body but loop back to your genitals, even if those parts aren't involved in the action.

What does sex mean to you?

We asked young people, parents and experts the question 'what is sex?' and we got heaps of different answers:

When I was 16 I'd learned 'what sex is' from movies and school. It was ALL about 'a man entering a woman'. I know sex is so much more than this now. For example, same-sex couples have sex! One really dangerous thing about this narrow-minded approach is a person may not know what something like sexual assault is. *Meghan, 21*

We keep hearing messages that tell us 'this is the next thing you're supposed to do' (with sex). But it would be good to acknowledge that sex doesn't have to happen in this order. You can skip things, stop anywhere. *Dr Jacqui Hendriks, sexologist*

A **SEXOLOGIST** IS SOMEONE WHO STUDIES RELATIONSHIPS AND SEX.

Sex is any kind of sexual act, including masturbation, that you do with your body. *Casper, 20*

Sex is a type of physical interaction between at least two people that is consensual. It's also a really good sort of stress relief that can be very healthy. *Lisa, 23*

Sex is any sexual activity including, but not limited to, penetrative sex and can also include non-physical activity like online sex. *Holly, 24*

I know sex is different for different people. But for me, I do think sex feels different when there's an (emotional) attachment. *Christian, father of two teens*

For me, sex is intimacy. For other people, intimacy might not be a factor. It means different things to different people. For some of my friends, video sex is their main form of intimacy. I didn't know what that would be like for me; I decided against it. *Dominique, 17*

Sex is something that feels mature when you're a teen. It can be scary, and it can be very enjoyable and intimate. It depends on who it's with; if it's the 'wrong' person it can hurt your body and your mind. *Grace, 18*

What is sexual pleasure?

Sexual pleasure is a way to describe physical sensations that are satisfying, enjoyable or thrilling, *and* positive emotions you feel from doing something sexual. So what makes it different from regular pleasure? It's all about the circumstances. A kiss on the cheek from your mum or a friend can feel nice, and it's a lovely way to connect. But it's very different when the kiss comes from someone you've got the hots for. Especially if you've been making meaningful eye contact all afternoon, they smell good, and you're starting to suspect they may like you back! When THEY lean over and kiss you on the cheek, you die of happiness and your **body tingles** all over.

> I now think of sex as a way to connect with someone that's pleasurable. People can do it for different reasons. *Fatema, 25*

Our bodies and brains are wired before birth to prepare us for sexual pleasure. You might have noticed that little kids play with their genitals (or 'private parts') because it *feels*

good. (You might have once been that little kid!) When we go through puberty, things turn up a few notches.

You are the captain of your pleasure

The thing about pleasure is that no-one else can tell you whether you did or didn't experience it. They may detect evidence, like sighs of happiness or snorts of laughter, but you are the sole owner of your feelings. Only YOU know if something is right or wrong for you, and what you felt.

This means that your own feelings are the best guide for what is 'good' for you sexually – and what is not. Checking in with your feelings to ask yourself:

Do I like this?

Am I enjoying this?

Does this feel good?

These feelings are crucial in having fulfilling and fair sex.

13

Why does pleasure matter?

Pleasure is something we all deserve and enjoy. Yay to feeling good! Most of us experience pleasure in all kinds of everyday situations – whether it's scratching an itchy leg, eating our favourite food, hanging out with mates or having a tidy room.

SEXUAL PLEASURE MATTERS BECAUSE IT'S ONE OF THE MAIN REASONS PEOPLE HAVE SEX. **FEELING GOOD** IS WHAT GETS PEOPLE DOING THIS STUFF. AND SEXUAL PLEASURE CAN BE ONE OF THE BIG PAYOFFS FOR MAKING IT SAFELY TO ADULTHOOD!

MORE ON p. 22

But talking about sexual pleasure can be a bit taboo. That's because lots of older people find it scary to think of young people (particularly young GIRLS) caring about getting pleasure, and being the bosses of getting pleasure. It's scary because it goes against what they were taught.

But the thing is, times have changed. Taboos around talking about sex are shrinking. And even the most uptight oldies are starting to understand that the best way for L-platers to navigate safe and respectful sex is for them to know exactly what turns them on and makes them feel good.

In sex there's no right or wrong way to do that – there's just what you like, what you're willing to try or experiment with, and what you don't like. Pleasure can be an excellent guide: 'Is this pleasurable?' 'Am I experiencing pleasure right now?' 'What about the other person?' 'Are we both getting pleasure from this experience?' That can help set the boundaries for what you will and won't do sexually.

It can be your starting point: 'Does this feel good for me?'

And if another person is involved:

Does this feel good for both of us?

Good question!

When experiences are new or really exciting, it's hard to know what the heck is going on with our feelings. We can be overwhelmed with joy *and* fear – not to mention loveheart-eyes and horniness! It can be A LOT. Trying to disentangle everything that's going on in our racing hearts and screaming minds is a big ask.

Some things are obvious. If a person kisses you and you don't like them? Your body might react with nausea. But what about someone you kinda *don't* like, who caresses your thigh in a way that feels good? What then?

When emotions are heightened, we like to do a mental pat-down.

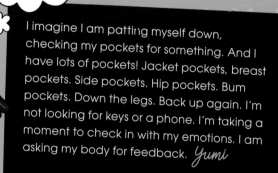

I imagine I am patting myself down, checking my pockets for something. And I have lots of pockets! Jacket pockets, breast pockets. Side pockets. Hip pockets. Bum pockets. Down the legs. Back up again. I'm not looking for keys or a phone. I'm taking a moment to check in with my emotions. I am asking my body for feedback. *Yumi*

Think: Am I OK? Does this make me feel good?

If you don't know the answer, then maybe you need to take a breather. Or maybe you need to stop.

In this situation, it is totally OK to say, 'I don't know what's going on, but I need a minute.'

If someone else is with you, you can ask them: 'Are you OK? Are you feeling good?'

Ask yourself: 'Is there anything I can do here to feel – or make the other person feel – safer, more at ease, happier?'

TIMES WHEN YOU MIGHT NEED TO DO A MENTAL PAT-DOWN

- ⭐ When you're panicking.
- ⭐ When it's something new.
- ⭐ When you feel like there's a roaring in your ears.
- ⭐ When you can't tell if it's fear or excitement.
- ⭐ When you're breathless or hot.
- ⭐ When you don't know if you can stop, but you think you should.
- ⭐ When you're experiencing pain or discomfort.
- ⭐ Anytime you feel stressed.

Why do people have sex?

Here are some reasons why people have consensual sex*:

- ⭐ Curiosity
- ⭐ It's fun and pleasurable
- ⭐ To share something intimate
- ⭐ It's romantic
- ⭐ They're in love
- ⭐ They're horny
- ⭐ They're super attracted to each other

- ⭐ To get pregnant
- ⭐ It's exciting
- ⭐ To bond
- ⭐ Stress relief
- ⭐ To help get to sleep
- ⭐ Relaxation
- ⭐ Exercise
- ⭐ Trying something new or experimenting

*Consensual sex means two (or more) people mutually deciding to have sex because they want to, and nobody feels forced or coerced by the other.

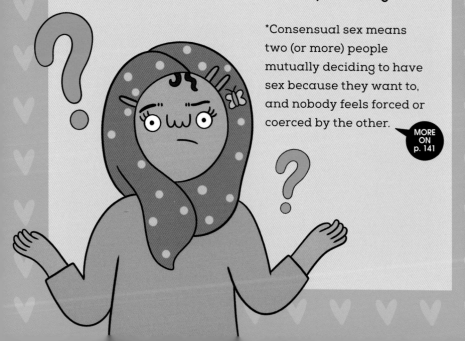

MORE ON p. 141

People have sex for crappy reasons, too. Sometimes they're motivated by insecurity. The logic goes, 'If I have sex with another person, maybe it will make them like me – or maybe I'll feel better about myself.' But it can do the opposite, and it doesn't fix insecurity. Reasons can get nasty too, like wanting to hurt your ex by having sex with another person. When we choose to have sex for these negative reasons, it can make sex much less enjoyable or, worse still, leave one or all people involved feeling bad, used or disrespected.

Teens we spoke to talked about feeling pressure to be 'grown-up' or 'cool' by having sex when it's not really what they wanted. It got especially complicated for young women, who can feel like they're walking a tightrope. They're trying to avoid being shamed for not being experienced without being shamed for having 'too much' experience.

I'm not too set (about when a person decides they want to have sex). I've chosen to wait, not because I see sex as a threat or a problem, but because I want to know a fair bit about something before I jump into it. *Jane, 22*

(At school,) it was completely different for guys. Boys who slept around were OK. There was a lot of peer pressure to have sex; girls had to have had sex but not have had too many partners. *Natalie, 28*

A lot of the time, the social pressure to have sex focuses on heterosexual, penis-in-vagina sex. This means LGBTQIA+ teens end up feeling excluded or distressed. They might feel pressure to have sex with a person they're not attracted to, and also to pretend to be someone they're not.

At age 16 I had my first girlfriend, a Lebanese Catholic girl. She did not want to have sex until she was married, which suited me as I didn't want to have sex with her. I would go home and cry and pray that God would make me feel attracted to women. *Bee, from the podcast One Foot In*

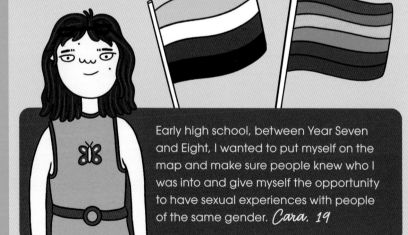

Early high school, between Year Seven and Eight, I wanted to put myself on the map and make sure people knew who I was into and give myself the opportunity to have sexual experiences with people of the same gender. *Cara, 19*

I think that in a young person's world it can start to be a sort of rat race, a rite of passage to experience sex, sort of this pressure, not only from peers now but also all the social media, TikTok. All of these outside things where you know you're not cool if you haven't (had sex). *Lisa, 23*

It can be hard to figure out what YOU want to do when there's all this pressure around. But part of being an adult is learning to tune in to the voice inside of you to figure out what will make YOU happy. And this book is here to help with that.

I didn't get into a relationship during high school and I think it's important to emphasise that it's OK to delay if you think you're not ready. There might be a lot of pressure to get into a relationship. If your friends are getting into one, it doesn't mean that you have to, and you don't have to do it just because it might be the 'cool' thing to do. *Fatema, 25*

If sex is so great … why is it so hard to talk about?!

There were actually times in ancient history when it WASN'T hard to talk about sex! Nowadays, talking or even *thinking about talking* about sex can bring up uncomfortable feelings for some people, such as shame, fear, awkwardness or embarrassment. We inherit strong beliefs about sex from our family, culture, religion and society.

Many people believe sex is private or sacred, and it's offensive or crass to discuss it openly. Adults might worry that if kids hear about sex, they will no longer be 'innocent'. Because of these taboos, people struggle to admit that sex is pleasurable and natural. Maybe for some adults it hasn't been so pleasurable.

It's understandable that these concerns would make adults feel protective of children and teens. But we're guessing that you are naturally **curious** about sex.

LEARNING ABOUT SEX WILL **NOT** MAKE YOU GO AND LOOK FOR SEX IF YOU'RE NOT READY.

Some deeply held and uncool ideas about sex are applied differently to women, and to disabled people, or those who are not cisgender and heterosexual. Teens who identify as LGBTQIA+ or who are simply figuring out their sexuality can feel very excluded or outright discriminated against.

NONE OF THIS IS OK!

It's time to break down the myths and taboos that have held some people hostage to rigid beliefs about sex.

Being sexual bonds us, it makes us feel good, it connects us – but what happened in history is that humans separated sex from other good human attributes. Sex was seen as this base, animalistic thing … it became kind of 'bad'. *Jacqueline Hellyer, sex therapist*

A **SEX THERAPIST** IS A SPECIALISED PROFESSIONAL COUNSELLOR WHO TALKS TO PEOPLE ABOUT SEXUAL WORRIES AND CONCERNS.

I thought of 'sex organs' as dirty, taboo. My mother would shame boys for touching their penises from a young age. My brother told me that if I masturbated, I wouldn't grow taller. *Bee, from the podcast One Foot In*

PARENTS AND CARERS AND AWKWARD CONVERSATIONS

...

My parents have NO IDEA

This statement is backed by loads of research! Surveys ask a bunch of teens if they're having sex, and then ask their parents if their kids are having sex. The teens say YES and the parents say NO – meaning, teens are having sex but their parents think they're not.

> I'm 40 and I still haven't ever talked to my parents about sex in detail.
> *Rocio Marte, 40*

Plenty of teens do want their parents or carers to be more clued in. Others worry that their folks will be disappointed or angry. Some think their parent or carer will stop them from seeing the person they're having sex with.

You probably get that your parents want the best for you, even if it means having tricky conversations or getting into arguments. Your mum, dad or carer could be super worried that you're not ready, or that you'll get hurt. And *disclaimer* there will be situations where your safety does come first and you legally aren't able to consent. But as you grow up, your sex life and your sexuality belong to you alone, and wanting privacy is healthy and natural. How much you want others to know, whether it's a parent or a buddy, is ultimately up to you. What we can say is that in *most* families, conversations about sex where parents listen well (even if they voice their worries or opinions) are important on many levels. Such discussions are supportive, caring and good for your sexual health! It also means that if something goes weird, they understand where you're at and might be in a better place to support you.

MORE ON p. 277

There are some teens with a genuine fear of a serious reaction if their parents find out they're having sex. It might be unsafe, involve being kicked out of home, or being shamed in their family or community. If this is you, there are safe places you can turn to for more advice.

MORE ON p. 285

How do I talk to my parents about sex?

I love this question. It's usually parents or carers who ask me, 'How do I talk to my teen about sex?' So when a teen asks this question, it strikes me as mature, caring and ... well, brave. It's probably fair to assume that for most teenagers, bringing up the topic of sex with a parent is, um ... awkward. *Dr Melissa*

Reasons you might want to talk to your parents/carers about sex:

* ⭐ **You want an honest conversation about whether you're ready**

* ⭐ **You want to tell your parents/carers that you've started having sex**

* ⭐ **You want their advice about being safe**

* ⭐ **You know they give good relationship advice**

* ⭐ **You're curious, worried or scared**

* ⭐ **You want to talk to an adult who really cares about you**

* ⭐ **You want to understand their values or beliefs when it comes to sex**

* ⭐ **You need support getting birth control**

Remember, your parents/carers were once teens too! Chances are they will know exactly how you feel and want to put you at ease, even if the topic makes them feel weird about how fast you're growing up.

STARTING THE CONVO:

⭐ Be upfront about how awkward it is: 'Hey, this is a bit weird for me but I really want to talk to you about sex. Is that OK?'

⭐ Give out some hints and see if they'll notice: 'There was this weird sex scene on (insert name of TV show)!' or 'Did you see that news story about teenagers and sex?'

⭐ Mention sex ed at school, and say that there are things you want to learn more about: 'We learned how to put a condom on a banana at school today … um, they forgot to teach us how to talk to your parents about sex!'

⭐ Talk honestly about how you're feeling: 'I'm really confused/scared/excited about sex. Can we talk about it?'

> One of my friends had sex very young and I remember telling my mum straight away, like, 'What the hell is happening?' *Izzy, 19*

Talking to parents

I don't think I ever discussed sex in detail with my parents. I never had 'the talk' of 'this is what sex is'. As I got older and people started to have sex I always felt very awkward talking to my parents about it! *Tiger, 19*

You could NEVER tell your parents, you were TERRIFIED of the idea of your parents finding out that you'd kissed someone, and you were so nervous about it! *Izzy, 19*

Sex can involve all sorts of different feelings. My advice to teens who are talking to parents would be – try to ask about and explain, how you're feeling. *Bibi, mother of four teens*

As a parent, I think, 'It's going to happen whether I know about it or not. It's out there – porn, fetishes, stories in the playground.' I let my kids know that they can talk to me. *Christian, father of two teens*

My parents had always told me sex was about an emotional connection and then I got to this school and everyone was joking and being so crass. This confused me and made me feel like I didn't know how to talk about sex. *Charlotte, 17*

When I was in Year Six my parents sat us down with the *Where do Babies Come From?* book and we had the Official Sex Talk. If you have a cool, young aunt, you can ask her about sex. Older cousins can be good sources of information. But even the coolest parents, who are the most understanding? I think there's a block there. *Gemma*

I was lucky to have my nan. She gave me resources to read. She didn't hide anything. I went to my nan rather than my dad. *Jessie, 23*

GETTING INTIMATE WITH MYSELF

How are you supposed to enjoy sex with another person if you don't know how to feel pleasure by yourself? Figuring out what feels good for YOU means you can bring that understanding to any future sexual experiences! You also have the right to feel pleasure on your own, regardless of when or if you ever have sex with another person. So let's start here: **with you!**

As a kid (I used to lie) on the couch rubbing against a pillow. I would've been about eight or nine and I had discovered this position where I lay like a frog and put pressure against myself! I remember showing my friend and she was like, 'I don't get it.' *Gemma*

❝ When I watched this horny movie I got twinkles, what is it down below? **❞**

❝ I have strong urges ... and pleasure myself about three times a day. I'm wondering if this is normal? **❞**

❝ When I was little I used to play 'sex' as a game with my friends. We used to rub our bodies together. **❞**

Twinkles, tingles, urges ... these are some of the words teens have used to describe sexy, pleasurable sensations. But these feelings aren't new – babies and little kids discover very early on that when they touch some parts of their bodies, it feels good!

When puberty hits, surges of **hormones** intensify these pleasurable feelings.

And your body might even feel these sensations *without* touch – it can react to sexy thoughts, fantasies or images. Even when you're asleep and dreaming. No wonder it's an exciting, hectic time of life! Other ways to describe what's happening are feeling 'hot', 'horny' or 'turned on'. Doctors or health professionals might call it 'sexual arousal'.

I didn't understand what being horny was! So I would go and do exercise! I still avoid getting horny. If I'm busy and I feel horny I just ignore it. It's such a low priority in my life. It takes too much of my time! *Ramona, 17*

Many teens would like to know a whole lot more about what feels good. This takes time – and what feels good can change, whether you're by yourself or with another person.

I had to read a book to know how to touch myself! I didn't talk about ANY of this with my friends back then. *Rocio Marte, 40*

The puberty roller-coaster

Puberty makes your body, thoughts and emotions change dramatically. You can feel out of control! There's a massive physical growth spurt and your body can do things it never could before, including experiencing sexual arousal. There's a brain-power boost too – you might not realise it, but you learn to figure out problems differently and you get better at empathising with other people. (Which might make sex better for you and the person you're with!)

In puberty you want to hang out with your friends more, and you're figuring out who you are in the world. This complex and wild roller-coaster ride helps get you to adulthood.

Teens have told us that biology and sex ed classes teach them about the organs needed for 'reproduction' (aka making babies), but not about all the other ways our body parts are designed to make sex pleasurable. So let's look at that now!

Body bits – the genitals, aka 'private parts'

Our bodies come in a diverse range of shapes, sizes and abilities – and so do our 'private parts'. Here's the lowdown on what they are, what they can do and why they can bring us pleasure.

Genitals are sometimes called the 'external sex organs'. The genitals are at the lower end of the pelvic area, between the legs. They connect with other, inside bits called the 'internal sex organs'. And they all have a major role to play when it comes to sexual pleasure.

> (When I was in high school) I wanted to learn about what parts of your body can do, what things are pleasurable. *Casper, 20*

> In school sex ed, I found it really offensive to separate boys and girls. People should be universally educated. It's no wonder men can't find the clitoris! *Dominique, 17*

The medical names of these genital body bits are: vulva, (tip of the) clitoris, vaginal opening, penis and scrotum. It's also fine to use words like 'front hole' for vagina. Some people prefer 'erectile tissue' when referring to their penis or clitoris. And some people are most comfortable calling everything 'genitals' (see Words, words, words on page 46).

INTERSEX VARIATIONS

Did you know ... genitals are identical in all human fetuses for the first nine weeks? After this, a baby's chromosomes and hormones start to influence how their genitals develop and grow. The size, shape and appearance of our genitals also change a lot during puberty.

When a baby is born, one of the first things the parent/s, support people, midwives or doctors do is look at its genitals. The adults surrounding the squawking, slippery little bub are often in a huge hurry to make a classification of its sex, and will usually decide that it's female or male.

Some people are born with what's called an intersex variation. This can be a variation in the genitals, other reproductive organs, hormones or chromosomes, or a combination. Usually, these variations are not noticeable when a baby is born. They (or their parents or doctors) might only find out later in life, such as when they go through puberty. It's estimated that about 1.7 per cent of people have an intersex variation – that's almost two in a hundred! Many intersex people are given hormones or have surgery done to change their genitals when they are children without their knowledge or consent. This is an abuse of their rights and bodily autonomy.

What genitals look like in a fetus for the first 2– 3 months

Genitals starting to develop more in the fetus after 2 - 3 months

A FEW EXAMPLES OF GENITAL DIVERSITY

Female genitals

VULVA

The vulva is a collection of different structures that make up what we call the 'female genitals'. A vulva doesn't stick out like our nose or big toe, or ... a penis. Instead it's tucked between the legs, not getting in anyone's way. But the vulva is incredible! It has all these parts:

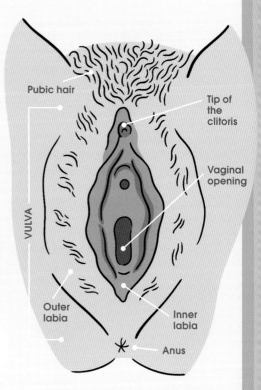

Pubic hair

Tip of the clitoris

Vaginal opening

VULVA

Outer labia

Inner labia

Anus

OUTER LABIA

LABIA = LIPS ...
DOCTORS THINK
WE SPEAK LATIN!

Two puffy little cushions that will grow pubic hair during puberty. They meet in the middle at the top, in front of your pubic bone. That soft little mound is called the mons pubis (Latin for 'mound or mountain on the pubic bone').

INNER LABIA

Soft flaps or strips that sit 'behind' or inside the outer labia. They come in all sorts of beautiful shapes and sizes and can look like petals. Their edges can go beyond the outer labia, so that if you pull your pants down and look at the vulva with a mirror, you'll see both the outer and inner labia. Some inner labia are fully inside the outer labia, so you can't see them until you spread the outer labia apart.

The skin covering the inner labia is different to the outer labia's. It has lots of nerve endings that can react to touch and feel pleasurable or sexy. The inner labia doesn't grow hair. Instead, it has lots of tiny glands that make an oily substance to keep the labia smooth. The inner labia meet in the middle at the top to form a little hood for the tip of the clitoris.

WHAT DO OTHER PEOPLE'S LABIAS LOOK LIKE?

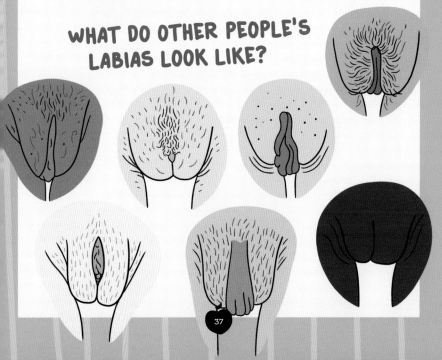

CLITORIS

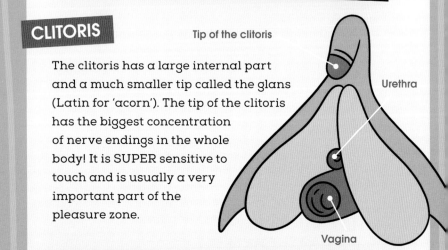

Tip of the clitoris

Urethra

Vagina

The clitoris has a large internal part and a much smaller tip called the glans (Latin for 'acorn'). The tip of the clitoris has the biggest concentration of nerve endings in the whole body! It is SUPER sensitive to touch and is usually a very important part of the pleasure zone.

THE INTERNAL CLITORIS

It wasn't until the mid-1990s that an Australian doctor called Professor Helen O'Connell fully figured out the structure of the clitoris. She found that the whole clitoris has several parts that swell up when you get turned on. The tip is the only part you can see from the outside. The rest of the clitoris is on the inside, and wraps itself around the vagina and urethra. It's why being touched or rubbed inside the vagina (with fingers, a penis or a sex toy, for example) feels good. There's an area inside the vagina that can be ultra-sensitive. It's a place that was once called the 'G-spot' but is now known to be part of the clitoris.

VAGINA

The vagina is a long muscular tube from the uterus to the outside world. It's where babies come out when they're born. Some people may be born without a vagina or with a short vagina. The opening of the vagina is part of the vulva, but most of it is inside the body and you can't see it. The opening is the most sensitive to touch and stimulation.

HYMEN

At the opening of the vagina there is usually a thin piece of tissue called the hymen. It's a similar colour to the inner labia. The hymen is a leftover piece of tissue from when the person was just a fetus, and their vagina, uterus, bladder and urethra were forming. The hymen doesn't serve any purpose after this, but it usually doesn't disappear completely. If you spread apart the labia at the opening of the vagina, you might see it. It can look like a sliver of skin or it might be larger – like a very thin sheet of skin with an opening in it.

The hymen and its opening come in many shapes and sizes. As a child grows, the hymen shrinks in size and its opening gets bigger. Once puberty hits, it shrinks even further.

WHAT DO
OTHER PEOPLE'S
HYMENS
LOOK LIKE?

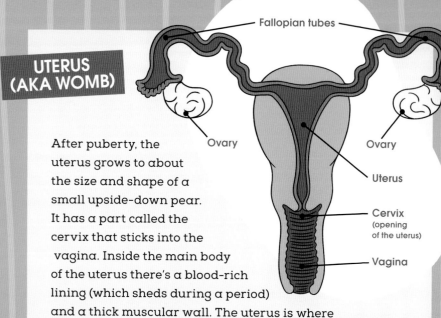

Fallopian tubes

UTERUS (AKA WOMB)

Ovary

Ovary

Uterus

Cervix
(opening
of the uterus)

Vagina

After puberty, the uterus grows to about the size and shape of a small upside-down pear. It has a part called the cervix that sticks into the vagina. Inside the main body of the uterus there's a blood-rich lining (which sheds during a period) and a thick muscular wall. The uterus is where a fetus grows into a baby. When someone with a uterus has an orgasm the uterus muscles go into slow, rhythmic contractions, which can feel very pleasurable.

MORE ON p. 67

FALLOPIAN TUBES

These are special tubes that carry eggs released by the ovaries towards the uterus. They are lined with tiny hair-like structures that help the eggs move along.

FEMALE GENITAL MUTILATION

Female genital mutilation (FGM, sometimes called female genital cutting) is when some parts of the genitals are removed, usually when the child is young. It can involve removing some or all of the clitoris tip and hood, and inner and outer labia. This has been practised in some cultures for many centuries but is illegal now in most other countries, because of its inherent violence and because it causes long-term health effects.

These are egg-making factories. During most of the years that a person has periods, these tiny powerhouses take turns each month to ripen an egg and release it into the Fallopian tubes.

Male genitals

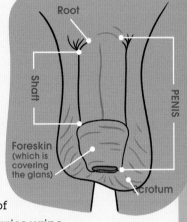

Root

Shaft

PENIS

Foreskin (which is covering the glans)

Scrotum

PENIS

Unlike the vulva, the penis often needs no introduction. The penis sticks out from the pelvic area. People with a penis are usually well acquainted with it from a young age, because they need to hold and steer it for one of its main functions – peeing. It carries urine from the bladder to the outside world through the urethra, which opens at or close to its tip. Apart from that, the inside of the penis is mostly full of 'spongy' tissues that fill up with blood during an erection (see Pleasure zone on page 49).

A penis has a root (think 'tree root', nothing else!), which is the part attached to the pelvic area. The longer middle part of the penis is called the shaft or body and the tip is called the glans. The skin of the penis does not have hair, but does have the same oil-producing glands found in the inner labia. It has nerve endings that help with sexual arousal, and these are especially sensitive on the penis glans.

SCROTUM & TESTICLES

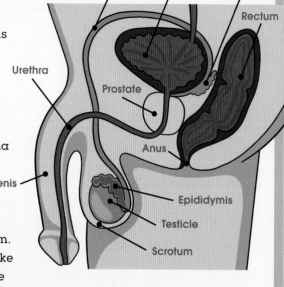

Vas deferens   Bladder   Seminal vesicle

Rectum

Urethra

Prostate

Anus

Testicles   Penis

Epididymis

Testicle

Scrotum

The scrotum holds the testicles, or 'balls'. It's like a hairy sac – it grows pubic hair during puberty, like the outer labia of the vulva.

Testicles usually come in pairs and live inside the scrotum. They're shaped like ovals. You can see the scrotum outside the body, hanging under the penis like a wrinkly skin sac. Right before puberty, the testicles are smaller than a 20 cent coin. They more than quadruple in size during puberty (!) and get to about the size of golf balls. The testicles are the sperm factories of the body. Sperm are made inside testicles and then stored in stored in long, coiled tubes called the epididymis. Inside the epididymis, sperm become more mature and learn how to swim! During ejaculation (see Orgasms on page 64), the sperm are transported in a liquid called semen through tubes called the vas deferens into the urethra and out through the penis. The liquid in semen comes from the testicles, the prostate gland and the seminal vesicles. These extra fluids keep the sperm nourished, ready for their big swim.

CIRCUMCISED/UNCIRCUMCISED

At birth, a penis is covered by a 'hood' of skin called the foreskin. In some cultures, it's customary to remove the foreskin within the first few days of being born. This is called (male) circumcision. In In the UK & Ireland today, most babies with penises do not have their foreskin removed, and are 'uncircumcised'.

CHECKING YOUR BALLS

It's good to get into the habit of regularly checking your testicles for lumps (sometimes called a 'testicular self-examination'). Most lumps that might appear in a teenager's testicles aren't too serious. But unlike some other cancers, cancer of the testicles is more common in younger people.

It's best to do it when your balls and scrotum are warm, such as in the shower. Check one thoroughly, then the other, using both hands to feel all the way around your balls. They'll feel like small, smooth eggs with a tube or bunch of tubes at the back of them. If you're ever worried that something's changed, or you just want reassurance, chat to a doctor about them.

My mum is a nurse and said if you're in the shower, along with normal stuff, like, 'actually clean behind your foreskin and occasionally check around your balls for bumps or foreign-feeling lumps'. *Seb. 19*

The parts we all have

URETHRA OPENING

The urethra is the tube that carries urine (pee) from your bladder to the outside world. In people with typically female genitals, the opening of the urethra is just below the tip of the clitoris. In people with typically male genitals, the opening is usually at the very tip of the penis, but it can be anywhere along the penis.

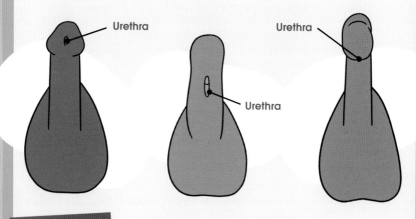

Urethra

Urethra

Urethra

PERINEUM

The perineum is the area between your anus and scrotum or vulva. It supports the pelvic floor and contains many nerves that support sexual function. This can be a highly sensitive area and pleasure centre.

ANUS This is where your poo comes out. It's a clever piece of equipment, too. An anus can usually tell when there's solid poo, liquid or gas waiting to get out – and it keeps tight control over the exit door! It does this because of lots of nerve endings sending messages between the brain and the muscles that open and close the anus. These nerve endings also make the anus sexually sensitive for many people.

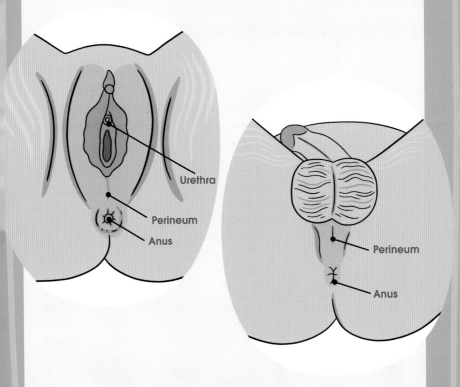

Urethra

Perineum

Anus

Perineum

Anus

Words, words, words

We often use nicknames for our genitals because we feel awkward or embarrassed about saying their actual names, which is understandable. But nicknames are also sometimes used in an offensive way, and that's *not* OK.

Here are some of the names and emojis people use for the 'private parts' of the body.

PENIS
doodle, dick, cock, JT (John Thomas), member, willy

VAGINA
fanny, front bottom, twot, mutte, munay, front hole

ANUS
bum hole, browneye

VULVA
lips, petals, flaps, fanny flaps, pussy

CLITORIS
clit, button, bean, sweet spot

TESTICLES
balls, eggs, nuts

SCROTUM
ball bag, ball sack, gurras

BREASTS
boobs, boobies, norks, knockers, melons, 80085 (on a calculator)

Sex ed experts say it's important to demystify all the words we use for genitals and sex organs, and we agree. They're just words! Learning to use their proper names will also clear up heaps of confusion – for example, in the USA, a 'fanny' is a bottom, but in Australia and the UK it's a vagina.

There's all this language in emojis – I didn't know them and some people misunderstood something I said to mean I wanted sex! I deleted all my social media for a while after that! *Natalie. 28*

If you're with a new partner, it's also important to check in about words or slang that you like or dislike to describe genitals and other body parts, and vice versa.

If a cisgender approaches a transgender, they must both learn to communicate about anatomy (body bits) and things like 'pet names' for body parts. I had a cisgender male partner who once referred to my body parts as 'tight' (and) 'not wet' – this caused me to feel dysphoria. *Casper. 20. trans male*

Pleasure zone

For most of us, the genitals are an awesome pleasure zone with super-sensitive nerve endings. When you're in the mood, any touch there can feel amazing!

There's special tissue built into genital parts called 'erectile tissue'. It's found inside the clitoris and the penis. When the genitals are touched, or if you're having sexy thoughts, blood flows into this tissue and it swells up. For people with a penis, this is called an erection. People with a vagina might notice clear liquid coming out – the increased blood flow causes the vagina to lubricate itself. The whole area can feel warm and 'tingly'.

When you're sexually aroused your heart rate goes up and your breathing gets faster. The skin in other parts of your body might get flushed or sweaty and feel warm; your nipples might get hard and your pupils might dilate.

Some people have different pleasure zones away from the genitals, especially if they have had a spinal injury or have a condition that affects the nerve supply to the sensitive genital area. Our incredible, adaptable human body means other parts can respond to sexy touch – such as earlobes, or the nape of the neck!

66 I have a really embarrassing problem –
sometimes I get erections when I'm at school.
It could be in class or during lunchtime and
it comes out of nowhere. Even just talking
about sex in our PE class can bring it on.
Is there any way I can stop it? 99

Erections do not always equal sexual arousal. Especially during the puberty years, when hormone levels fluctuate, erections can appear at random! To get rid of them, it can help to think about something decidedly unsexy, or take a cold shower (which sometimes works). Plenty of penis-owners of all ages often wake up with erections, too.

Exploring your body

Some people find it most pleasurable to touch their clitoris or penis directly, while others enjoy rubbing the whole genital area. Other parts of the body, a long way from the genitals, can also be 'erogenous zones', meaning they can turn you on sexually. The mouth, lips and nipples are common erogenous zones. Others are the neck, scalp, earlobes, small of the back, bum cheeks, thighs, belly button, hands, feet ... in fact, almost anywhere on the body! It all depends on what you're in the mood for or who's doing the touching. Your reactions can change each time.

When you're ready, use a small mirror and look at your genital area. You can lie on your bed, or stand or sit in the shower. Check out the whole area between the tops of your thighs, from the front pelvic bones, all the way to your anus (bum hole). This is your body and you are allowed to do this!

I was probably 14 when I first looked at my genitals. Someone had told me there were three holes and I was like, 'Where are they all?' so I got a mirror to have a look. I thought, 'That's cool!' Before that I thought maybe the pee-hole and vagina hole were the same thing. *Gemma*

If you have a vulva, separate the outer labia (lips), look at the opening of the vagina and the urethra, and find the tip of the clitoris, which usually hides underneath a 'hood'. If you have a penis, lift it up and look at where its base joins the scrotum. If you have testicles, get to know what they feel like. Knowing your body is the first step towards getting to know pleasure.

For some teens, looking at their genitals is distressing. One reason might be gender dysphoria – which is when your gender identity is different from the one that was presumed at birth (see Gender identity labels on page 77). There are other reasons people might feel uncomfortable looking at or touching their genitals. Only explore what makes you feel comfortable and emotionally safe.

I have used a mirror to look at my genitals. It's not super comfy to do. *Tiger, 19*

Masturbation

QUESTIONS FOR DR MELISSA

❝ I'm 16 and I get really horny all the time and when I do I don't exactly know how to turn myself on? Can you help and tell me how to, please? ❞

❝ A lot of my friends are talking about fingering so I was curious and I tried it. I'm 12 so I thought I'd be able to stick a finger up but I couldn't and it sort of hurt. Is there something wrong with me? ❞

❝ I'm a 15-year-old female who's feeling the urge for sex. I know I don't want to have intercourse just yet but I don't know of any ways to please this need?! Are there any techniques, or household items that I could use? And how? I don't own a vibrator so what else could I use? ❞

❝ I was wondering if it is normal to be horny, i.e. when my parents are not home I go to their room and play with the vibrator, which I stick up my vagina. What is wrong with me? ❞

Masturbation means touching your own body for sexual pleasure. It's a great way to discover the gifts your body can give you, and commonly involves touching your genital area with your hands. Sometimes masturbation will lead to an orgasm (but it isn't compulsory!).

An orgasm, also called a 'climax', is an intense feeling of pleasure. It is really common and perfectly OK to feel REALLY horny in your teenage years. Masturbation is a great way to let off steam, relax and explore your body and what feels good.

MORE ON p. 64

For over 20 years, I read hundreds of letters from teens about masturbation. I was asked a lot of questions – from how to do it, to how often you should do it, to how to deal with feelings of embarrassment or shame. Sometimes a young person will ask me a question about it when I see them in my clinic. Masturbation is common, it's safe and people of all genders do it! Dr Melissa

How to masturbate

DO NOT DISTURB

> I needed a bit of guidance. On school camp one of my friends told me about masturbation and I was like, 'WHAT IS THAT?' I'd obviously touched my penis before but never done that so I waited till I got home and tried … it was, like, WOAH. That was before I had gone through full puberty so there was no ejaculation but there was an orgasm. *Josh, 17*

The way you masturbate can change each time. For some people the process of masturbating to orgasm is sped up by thinking about something they find sexy. There's no specific formula for how to do this, and we creative humans have discovered lots of different ways! What feels really good one time can change the next time, so you might want to experiment with different techniques.

There is no correct way to masturbate, and you should do what feels good for you at the time.

Here are some of the ways people masturbate:

☆ **USING YOUR HANDS** to rub the sensitive parts of your body is a common and straightforward way to get turned on. This can be rubbing your fingers around your whole genital area or concentrating just on the most sensitive parts, such as the tip of the clitoris or penis.

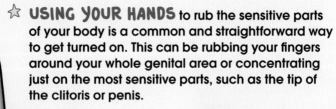

☆ **IF YOU HAVE A VULVA AND CLITORIS**, you can rub the whole or just part of the area up and down, side to side, in a circular motion or a combination. You can use saliva or lubricant to moisten the area, too. You might use one hand to rub your genital area and the other hand to play with your nipples, or to touch any other part of your body that feels nice. As you become more aroused, parts of your genitals will swell a little. The feelings of pleasure usually increase in intensity over a few minutes and can reach a climax, or orgasm. If that happens, hormones in the brain are released that can make you feel relaxed and happy.

MORE ON p. 64

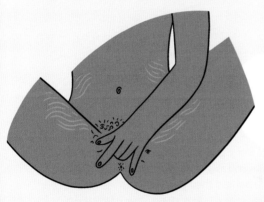

WASH YOUR HANDS BEFORE AND AFTER!

☆ **IF YOU HAVE A VAGINA**, it might become moist and leak clear fluid when you touch yourself. You can put one or more fingers inside your vagina – as far up as feels comfortable – and 'massage' the inside of it with your fingertips. You can use saliva or lubricant if it helps. If this is uncomfortable or doesn't feel good, then stop. You can wait and try again, or not. It doesn't mean anything's wrong.

☆ **IF YOU HAVE A PENIS,** rubbing your whole hand up and down the length (shaft) of the penis can help you get an erection, and also keeps up the stimulation. You can wrap several fingers or your whole hand around the shaft, and pull on it (gently!). Some people use some saliva or lubricant to moisten the tip of the penis, which can increase its sensitivity.

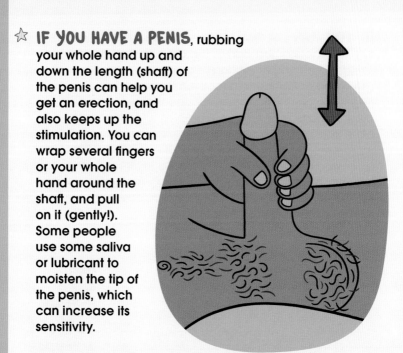

☆ Some people find it very pleasurable to be touched around their anus (bum hole). If you do, then make sure you've thoroughly washed that part of your genital area beforehand. After you touch this area, avoid putting your hands near the opening of your urethra (where pee comes out). This is because bacteria from your gut often lie on the skin around the anus, and if they get inside your urethra it could lead to a urinary tract infection. This is much more common in girls than boys, because a girl's urethra is much shorter than a boy's. (See Care and hygiene on page 62.)

Genital skin inside and out is sensitive. Wash your hands (and anything else you might use to touch your genital area) really thoroughly before you start! To moisten the genital area, only use saliva, lubricant or tap water. Avoid soaps, hand sanitiser, perfumes or other products that are not designed for use in the genital area, as they could irritate the skin and cause a rash, stinging or swelling.

Masturbating with objects

As well as fingers and hands, people might enjoy using objects to touch their genitals. There are special products that are designed to stimulate sexual pleasure – these are broadly known as 'sex toys'. In Australia it is illegal to sell them to anyone under 18. These products are designed to do things like: being put inside the vagina; vibrating around the genital area, on the clitoris or inside the vagina; or going inside the anus. Sometimes people discover household objects to play with (for example, a hairbrush handle, a pillow, a shower head). Use common sense – make sure anything you put INSIDE is clean, and don't use anything sharp or that might break!

❝ I am a 13-year-old boy and I am wondering, when should I start masturbating? My friends say that they do, but I'm not sure when I should. Please help. ❞

There's no right or wrong age to masturbate. Babies and little kids might do it, and old people might never have done it. Just because other people are talking about it, or say they're doing it, doesn't mean you have to. Masturbating and learning about pleasure should only happen on your own terms, if and when you're ready and you want to. You're the boss of your body!

❝ I have a problem; I masturbate ALL the time! Even when I'm in class I ask the teacher if I can go to the toilet and when I get there I finger myself. Can you tell me if there is something wrong with me and how can I stop?! ❞

Discovering this new thing that's so pleasurable and FREE can create a fair bit of chaos! There's no right or wrong to how often you masturbate – some kids do it almost never, others masturbate several times a day. If it feels like it's taking over your life – like you're skipping class to masturbate – then see if you can rein it in. If it's really starting to stress you out, there's confidential help out there (see Is something wrong? on page 260). But remember, you ARE in the middle of the hormone storm that is puberty, so don't think you're alone! And it won't be this intense forever.

We were playing one of those games, Never Have I Ever, and one of my mates said he'd masturbated nine times in a day! Masturbating to climax! I would guess that he probably had some sort of an addiction? Or maybe he was testing himself or whatever? *Seb, 19*

66 I want to know if you can damage your clit by rubbing it too much when you masturbate, and if it does get damaged will it stop you from having orgasms? **99**

If rubbing your clitoris is feeling good, nothing bad is happening! If it's starting to feel tender or painful, it's not because you're damaging it. It could be that you need more moisture, such as saliva or lubricant.

Or it could be a signal to slow down, take a break; maybe touch other sensitive parts of your body instead. Luckily, you can't damage your clitoris from having too many orgasms. Phew!

66 I'm 13 and haven't got my period yet and basically all my friends have. I do masturbate and am really scared that that's why I don't have it! I'm in a B cup and almost a C cup! Does masturbation stop your period?? Please help. **99**

Nope. Nah. Masturbate without fear! Your period will come about two years after you first noticed your breasts growing. And even if it comes a bit later than

that, it has nothing to do with masturbating.

66 Recently I was masturbating and I think my mum saw me. What am I going to tell her? Is it wrong to masturbate? HELP!!! **99**

You don't have to tell your mum about this if you don't want to. Masturbation is something you're entitled to do, and to keep private. *But*, if you want to, you could turn that moment of awkwardness into a conversation ... like, 'Hey Mum, this feels really weird, but can we talk about what happened the other day?' She's probably been wondering how to have a conversation with you about it, and about sex in general. Some parents feel awkward talking to their teens about sex. Others don't.

Here's the thing: your mum probably masturbated too when she was young, and chances are she's still doing it. It's not wrong to masturbate. In fact, it's very common; people of all genders and ages do it, including mothers, fathers and grandparents. It's quite good for you. So if your mum saw you, she was probably thinking, 'We've all been there!'

> **I'm circumcised, but heaps of my mates aren't. They say sex and masturbation feels better if you're not circumcised. Is that true?**

We'd like to know how your mates became such experts on other people's penises and pleasure. Have they done some research? Have they interviewed people with diverse penises?

The good news is: the research *has* been done – many times over – and the conclusion is that being circumcised (aka having your foreskin removed) makes no difference to sexual sensations and pleasure. Sexual pleasure is NOT a reason to be circumcised or uncircumcised. Removing the foreskin from the penis is something that happens in some countries and cultures when you're a baby. Other times it is done for medical reasons, such as having a constricted foreskin that won't pull back. This can cause recurring pain or difficulties peeing. Creams can be tried first, but circumcision can end up being recommended.

FUN FACT: THE STORY OF THE HUMBLE CORNFLAKE ...

Dr Kellogg and his brother invented Kellogg's Corn Flakes almost 130 years ago. Dr Kellogg looked after patients in a big hospital and believed that simple, wholesome food not only helped them back to physical health but was also good for everyone's morals. He was also COMPLETELY against masturbation or any type of sex, except to make babies. He thought that spicy or tasty foods would lead to sinful, sexual thoughts (not true) and also harm your gut, so inventing Corn Flakes was part of his efforts to get people to stop masturbating ...
by changing what they ate!

Care and hygiene

Your genital area works hard for you, so it deserves some basic care and hygiene. Here's how to look after your bits!

☆ **Genital skin is more sensitive to irritants in cosmetics, perfumes and other products, so avoid putting these anywhere on your genitals. No moisturiser, no 'odour control' products – nothing!**

☆ When you're in the shower, pay attention to the whole genital area, washing it with water and hypo-allergenic soap.

☆ If you have a vulva, wash between the outer and inner lips and gently around the hood of the clitoris. Don't put any soap or sprays of water inside the vagina – it's a self-cleaning wizard and douching (washing out the inside of the vagina with water) can cause an imbalance in its ecosystem.

☆ If you have a penis with a foreskin, gently pull the foreskin back and clean around the tip/glans of the penis with water and a bit of hypo-allergenic soap.

☆ Clean between your bum crack and around your anus with soap and water. This applies to everyone. Poo comes out of there, so give it a good, thorough wash.

☆ Wash your hands with soap at the end of it all.

ORGASMS

What is an orgasm?

An orgasm is a combination of physical and psychological sensations that build up as you get more and more 'turned on' (aka 'sexually aroused') until it **peaks** and you experience an intense, some say 'explosive', pleasurable feeling. The feeling might be concentrated in your genital area, the whole pelvic area or your whole body, and it might feel tingly, hot and like fireworks going off.

Immediately afterwards you might feel happy, ecstatic, satisfied, emotional, calm, relaxed or sleepy. The whole thing might last just a few seconds or a minute or so, although there can be slow, follow-up waves of pleasure that last much longer.

Another word that can mean 'orgasm' is **'coming'** or **'to come'**. Sometimes it's spelled **'cum'**, which can also mean the sticky stuff (aka semen) that comes out of a penis when it ejaculates. The vagina can also spurt fluid or cum inside itself during an orgasm. It might not be noticeable because there can already be a lot of natural lubrication and fluid inside the vagina as it gets turned on.

BTW: in people with a penis, an orgasm and ejaculation usually happen at the same time, but they don't have to. Sometimes the person might have an orgasm without ejaculating, or vice versa.

Are orgasms important?

Yes. No. Maybe. Not always. It depends!

Orgasm does not equal 'good sex' – it's part of a dessert menu and it doesn't guarantee sexual satisfaction. We are taught to chase after orgasms, or we look to porn and movies for representation, when actual sex is sweaty, messy, a mix of different fluids!
Chantelle Otten, psychosexologist

During masturbation, orgasm might be one of your main goals. (Because orgasms usually feel great!) But there can be minutes or hours of enjoyment and pleasure from discovering your body on your own without aiming for an orgasm. It's a bit like the saying 'it's the journey, not the destination' – you learn better if you don't set up narrow expectations by racing to orgasm.

There are different ways to have an orgasm, too – they can be 'mini', 'explosive', multiple, super quick, 'dry' (no ejaculation), very focused on one part of your genitals or felt all over your body.

Sex with another person can be unsatisfying or even boring if either (or both) parties insist it should end with an orgasm. Not all sex does! For some people, orgasms are very important. For others, not so much. Over-emphasising the importance of orgasm can sometimes mean other pleasures get ignored or neglected. Some people enjoy slow, mindful, 'spiritual' sex that can go for a long time. This sex may or may not end in orgasm. It's for good reason that LOADS of songs have been written about 'going slow' and 'why rush?'

When you're on your L-plates, or even if you've been 'on your full licence' for years, sexual pleasure and fulfilment happen in a ton of different ways.

The process of sex is more about sharing intimacy. Orgasm is definitely a goal you can work towards, but it's not a wasted opportunity if you DON'T reach orgasm. *Cara, 19*

Sex (between people) is more than pleasure and orgasms, it's about two or more people coming together to create a beautiful, wonderful experience. It should be a moment-by-moment thing. *Jacqueline Hellyer, sex therapist*

What's actually going on when you have an orgasm?

Your brain is the control tower for directing brain chemicals and hormones to feel excited. It's also responsible for making blood rush into your genital area. To get to an orgasm, there's usually been a build-up of all these chemical reactions in the form of sexual excitement. Your nipples usually go hard, your heart rate and breathing both get faster, and the muscles in your pelvic area tighten up.

When an orgasm happens, these pelvic floor muscles will contract and pulse, as well as your uterus, if you have one (which is why orgasms can sometimes help with period pain). Your hands and feet might also 'spasm', or stiffen up, and your pupils dilate.

There's often a kind of 'high' or emotional rush of pleasant feelings. Sometimes when you orgasm you make an almost involuntary noise – a big loud sigh, or 'Aaaahhhhhhh!' Or your orgasms might be completely silent. It's all OK!

How do I have an orgasm?

SO many teens have told me they've been disappointed, confused or anxious about 'the Big O'. TV, movies, porn and general nonsense about 'right' and 'wrong' ways to have an orgasm can mean their 'climax' is one big anticlimax. *Dr Melissa*

A great way to figure out orgasms is to do some exploring yourself! What turns you on, and what brings you to an orgasm, is very specific to you, and it changes. It changes as you age and can change from orgasm to orgasm – whether through masturbation or with another person.
(See Masturbation on page 52.)

Commonly, a lot of people get to orgasm by repeatedly touching, stroking, caressing or rubbing their clitoris or penis. They generally need to feel safe to get to orgasm.

Some people have an orgasm when they're asleep, while they're having a sexy dream, and it doesn't even involve touching their body. Some people might have an orgasm from, say, touching only their nipples, while others will want or need to touch some part of their genitals. Orgasms can happen in all sorts of bodies with all sorts of genitals, including those with an intersex condition (see Body and sex characteristic labels on page 79), and those who have a disability, or who have had female or male circumcision, sex reassignment surgery or a spinal injury.

Let's be real about female orgasms!

For centuries, girls, people have been brainwashed into thinking that men's pleasure is more important than women's! We've been told that female bodies are harder to bring to orgasm. And that the only 'right' way to orgasm was with a penis inside their vagina!

THIS IS ALL UNTRUE!

Firstly, women's pleasure is equally important as men's. No argument!

Secondly, most female bodies can orgasm easily – when treated right.

And finally – and one of the reasons why we wanted to write this book – NONE OF US are taught enough about the clitoris and women's sexual pleasure. It's not a mystery – it's just not taught! Research has shown that **most women have an orgasm by having the tip of their clitoris directly touched**, and NOT from having a penis, finger or toy going into their vagina. For some, the combo of something INSIDE the vagina AND having the clitoris rubbed (by themselves or by their partner) is super pleasurable. It can change each time. This idea that you MUST or SHOULD orgasm from vaginal penetration is a MYTH.

Wet dreams

66 I was wondering how often most guys have wet dreams? I'm 14 and had my first one about a month ago and another one this week. Also, up to what age do you get them? It'd be pretty embarrassing if I was staying at someone's place and it happened. 99

A wet dream is when you ejaculate or orgasm while asleep.

Anyone can have a wet dream, although not everyone does. A penis will ejaculate more fluid than a vagina, so those ones tend to be noticed more (because the sheets are wet or sticky in the morning). If this happens, you might want to wash your bedsheets, or it mightn't bother you to have a small wet spot on your PJs or bedding. Wet dreams might happen because of a sexy dream and might involve an orgasm ... or not. The person might wake up, or might not. They can happen more frequently during the teen years because the puberty hormones are on a wild roller-coaster ride. And they can continue until old age!

If you're wet-dreaming all over the place and are worried about people discovering the evidence, there are a few things you can do. One is to relax. Everyone knows this is part of being a teen, so ... don't sweat! Talk to your parent or carer. Learn how to wash and change your own bedsheets – a necessary life skill anyway!

If you're sleeping over at a mate's place? Also relax. Take a change of PJ pants and wear undies just in case. And talk to your mate before, or after, if it does happen. It might seem awkward but it's highly likely they've experienced the same situation!

I've only ever had one wet dream where I've actually ejaculated. I'd rather not say what it was about! Thankfully I was at home, sleeping in underwear, so it was pretty simple to clean up. *Josh, 19*

LABELS: SEXUAL AND GENDER IDENTITIES

Identity is more than your ID

Have you ever filled out a form where you're asked your name, age or gender? Sometimes you're asked which country you or your parents were born in, your occupation or religion. These things might be important to you, private, or things you're unsure about. They might be part of your identity.

Identity means how you define yourself as a person. It helps answer the question 'Who am I?' When you were a kid, your parents probably ran your life for you, which felt safe and normal. As a teen, hanging out with friends might become the new normal. Maybe you'll have more responsibilities, like babysitting younger siblings. You might question your folks and teachers about why things are a certain way and want more say over your life. And maybe you'll ask big questions about the world and your place in it. It's all part of figuring out your identity. It's actually a big deal!

Having my identity defined has grounded me and helped me understand myself. But that's not true for everyone. Some friends haven't labelled their sexual identity. *Casper, 20, trans male*

Through high school, there was a constant swarm of 'who likes who' and I didn't like anyone. I identified as asexual. I became part of that community and I didn't feel broken anymore. Later, after I left school, I identified as lesbian – I remember vividly realising I liked women. *Holly, 24*

Teenage years are difficult! It's enough that you're going through puberty and just wanna fit in, and then you put disability on top of that and it's another layer of being 'different'. I didn't always want to identify as disabled, I just wanted to fit in. Not that I didn't love being disabled. My friends and I would love to make jokes and play pranks on people. I had a prosthetic arm and we would leave it in peoples' lockers and backpacks and freak out the Year Sevens. *Madeleine, 28*

Sexual and gender identity

QUESTIONS FOR DR MELISSA

> I'm 13 and I'm really confused about my sexuality. I consider myself polysexual, but I'm still not sure. I hear a lot of people say, 'Oh you're just a kid, you don't know what you like,' and I don't know what to think anymore. Is it OK to be lesbian and straight at the same time?

Sexual identity and gender identity are some of the deepest parts of being a human – and they can change, too. Having a label for your sexual or your gender identity might be really important to you, or it might not. Some people find that having labels brings solidarity and connection with others. Others find labels unnecessary and feel boxed in by them. It's OK to use several different labels, or none at all!

Here are some of the more common labels that people use to express their sexual identity or their gender identity. Remember, labels are only for you to choose … no-one else!

It's not uncommon for people's sexual identity to change over time. Even though I write these books, I don't feel any need to announce my sexual identity to the world. It's my business. *Yumi*

Sexual identity labels

Your sexual identity is about how you define yourself sexually. It's usually about the gender of the people you feel sexually or romantically attracted to. Those attractions can change over time, or they might stay constant. There's no right or wrong – you're you!

GAY: I'm sexually and/or romantically attracted to people of the same gender as me. This label is used more commonly by males who are attracted to other males, but it is sometimes used by people of all genders.

BI/BISEXUAL: I'm sexually and/or romantically attracted to males and females.

HETEROSEXUAL: I'm sexually and/or romantically attracted to people of a different gender.

LESBIAN:
I'm female and sexually and/or romantically attracted to other females.

ASEXUAL:
I don't feel sexually attracted to any person, regardless of their or my gender.

AROMANTIC:
I don't feel romantically attracted to any person.

PANSEXUAL:
I'm sexually and/or romantically attracted to any or all genders; a person's gender doesn't figure in whether I'm sexually or romantically attracted to them.

Gender identity labels

Sex and gender – what's the difference? Sex is to do with the genitals, chromosomes and hormones we have, usually 'female', 'male' and 'intersex'. Gender is how we define ourselves as being female, male, neither, both or something else.

★ **CIS-FEMALE:** I identify as female and was presumed female at birth.

★ **CIS-MALE:** I identify as male and was presumed male at birth.

★ **GENDER FLUID:** I experience my gender identity as something that is not fixed; I may identify one way one day, and differently the next.

★ **TRANS-FEMALE OR TRANSGENDER FEMALE:** I identify as female and was presumed male at birth. Some transgender females identify as females (and don't use 'trans').

★ **TRANS-MALE OR TRANSGENDER MALE:** I identify as male and was presumed female at birth. Some transgender males identify as males (and don't use 'trans').

★ **NON-BINARY:** I experience gender as being outside two genders (female/male) and do not identify as just one or the other.

★ **AGENDER:** I don't identify with having a gender.

⭐ **SISTERGIRL/SISTAGIRL:** I'm an Aboriginal and/or Torres Strait Islander female who was presumed male at birth. I have a distinct cultural identity and often take on women's roles within the community. My cultural, spiritual and religious beliefs are pivotal to my life and identity.

⭐ **BROTHERBOY:** I'm an Aboriginal and/or Torres Strait Islander male who was presumed female at birth. I have a male spirit and a distinct cultural identity. My cultural, spiritual and religious beliefs are pivotal to my life and identity.

⭐ **QUEER:** This word fits with my sexual and/or gender identity. It means different things to different people.

'AROMANTIC' VS 'ASEXUAL'

The types of love and connection we want with people all vary. An aromantic person doesn't necessarily want or feel romantic love towards others. They might be happy in an intimate relationship with someone, but emotionally, the connection is more like a close friend. They might also want and enjoy sex with that person.

Being asexual means a person doesn't experience sexual attraction towards any people. An asexual person might, or might not, feel romantic love towards others.

Some people are aromantic AND asexual while others might be one or the other.

Body and sex characteristic labels

Hang on, what's a 'sex characteristic'?!

These are **physical** parts of your body related to genitals and reproductive organs, like the ovaries, clitoris, penis and scrotum (and many more). 'Sex characteristics' also refers to body parts that change due to puberty hormones, like growing boobs and pubic hair, getting rounded hips or getting a deeper voice (and many more things).

There's plenty of diversity when it comes to sex characteristics. We tend to learn about bodies being 'female' or 'male', and have standard ideas about what their body parts (both inside and out) look like. The label 'endosex' describes people whose sex characteristics align with these ideas.

'Intersex' is a whole bunch of ways that sex characteristics **vary** from the standard ones we think of as 'female' or 'male'. One example might be that someone has a body that looks male but has female reproductive organs inside (uterus, ovaries). Another example might be that someone has a female body but has an enlarged clitoris. Being intersex has nothing to do with sexual identity or gender identity. Someone who's intersex could identify in all the different ways that someone who's endosex might.

Coming out

Coming out is what happens when a person tells another person or people something about themselves that they had previously kept to themselves. It's about sharing part of your identity – usually sexual or gender identity. If you identify as cisgender and heterosexual, you might not ever think about wanting or needing to tell anyone. If you don't identify in these ways, then you might feel you need to come out.

For many teens, coming out can create anxiety about how others will react. I've met hundreds of teens over the years who have told me about what it was like for them to come out – to family, friends, school, work and broader society. This has varied from totally joyful and affirming to being really difficult. People's cultures, ethnicities, religions and societies can affect whether (and how) they choose to come out, and how safe they feel doing it. Teens should be able to choose who to come out to and when, but I know sometimes they get 'outed' by others. I wish we lived in a world where everyone knew they would be accepted no matter what – then no-one would ever feel they had to come out! *Dr Melissa*

My 12-year-old daughter told me that she likes girls. I said, 'It's wonderful, girls are so wonderful.' *Claire, mother of three teens*

I think if I ever came out to (my parents) that I was dating a woman, they would not want to speak to me anymore. I think for my parents, they can't deal with pain and maybe a partial factor (is) they're migrants from Vietnam, like, they already have to deal with so much culture shock in their life. They probably want some kind of uniformity – 'oh, you know, a man and a woman should be together'. They probably can't accept the fact that (some people) like same-gender people – it's just so foreign to them – like, 'the world is turning upside down, it can't be real'. *Lisa, 23*

I didn't make a big announcement. I just said 'I'm in a relationship' and (that) it was with a woman. I came out to my friends first. I didn't come out to my family until my relationship broke up and they knew I was upset. They were supportive. I wished I'd come out earlier – I felt bad that I had been lying. *Holly, 24*

Teens and adults who have come out have shared tips for those who are wondering about it. Here are some of them (see More resources on page 294 for more info):

★ **Choose the time that's right for you – there's no rush.**

★ **Identify someone who will support you.**

★ **If you're worried about someone's reaction, you can test it out by bringing up the topic indirectly first.**

★ **Figure out how you'll do it, and maybe talk it through with someone. Write out the words you'll say, or what you'll post on social media; do you want something low-key or a big blast?**

★ **Remember that for lots of us, coming out can be an ongoing process. Every time we meet a new person, start a new job? We might need to come out. So you get better at it, more relaxed, and the stakes can feel lower as you get older.**

I didn't have a 'worry moment' that I could be disowned or any of those things. My parents openly expressed that they're full of acceptance and joy and, you know, all the positives. Growing up, I knew it was always fine. *Lauren French (she/her), sexologist, sexuality educator and proud bisexual and First Nations woman*

I told my friends I was bi and they totally forgot! They just didn't care. And it's not a big deal. *Ramona, 17*

COMING OUT: TIGER'S STORY

My parents found out I was trans at the end of Year Eight – they could see I was quite depressed and they pointed out my self-harm scars and were obviously concerned about that. I wasn't planning on telling them for a while so it took a lot of prodding to say, 'I don't feel like a girl.'

They were really good about it and got me into therapy to talk that through with somebody who wasn't a parent because I was never very good at opening up in that sense.

With friends at school it was hard because it was an all-girls school. Even if I did tell people, it wasn't like they could immediately start changing their language!

When I started at a new school, most people perceived me as a guy. And most people I made friends with were queer in some way and really accepting.

It is an ongoing thing and at uni it has been hard to gauge who is a good person to come out to and who is not. I'm out to all my immediate friends and there's still a lot of people who I have chosen not to engage with. Even if they're good people, the education on trans issues is so minimal I know a lot of people won't understand. I know they might start perceiving me as a girl. It takes a lot of energy.

Try to build a tight-knit support group of your close friends or family, or people that you know you (can) always lean on, if you have certain situations where you can't come out because you know people will react badly. Having those people close to you who know who you are and are going to treat you right and be there for you is really important. Coming out can definitely feel like an isolating experience a lot of the time. You can feel like the odd one out. *Tiger, 19*

WHAT THE OUTSIDE WORLD IS TELLING US ABOUT SEX

There are plenty of outside influences that affect our attitudes towards sex, and we're going to take a look at the major ones. Remember, though: what YOU think about sex is ultimately up to you!

Young people figure out pretty quickly that sex can feel really good – physically and emotionally. Over the years, many teens have told me that they feel judged when it comes to their sexuality, simply because they're young. That can create a lot of guilt and shame. If they're not straight/heterosexual, or if they're female, trans or gender diverse, there can be multiple layers of judgemental attitudes. *Dr Melissa*

Modern culture and society

Many countries are now better at understanding human rights when it comes to sex and sexuality.

Gender equality, same-sex marriage, the rights of trans and gender-diverse young people, and laws about sexual consent are examples of our modern society recognising every person's right to equality as well as freedom from discrimination and violence. But there is still plenty of work to be done. In some places, human rights are actually being rolled back, particularly around abortion and birth control. While there might be widespread acceptance that young people can and will have sex long before they get married (something that has changed dramatically in only two generations!), some people are being forced to birth unwanted pregnancies, even if it puts their lives at risk.

Teenagers don't always feel that their rights are understood or respected. They still hear a lot of negative messages about sex. Sometimes teens themselves continue the ancient tradition of shaming girls' sexual behaviour. Or harass or bully other teens who are trans, non-binary or not heterosexual.

Let's be better! Young people have always been the ones to change the world. We can all imagine a world where everyone has the right to be who they are!

It's something that we've grown up with, misogyny and all these patriarchal beliefs – those thoughts don't come out of thin air! If we don't create change now, our younger sisters (and) nieces (will) think the same thing and it's not a great thing to feel! *Sahib, 15*

Religion

Religious beliefs help a lot of us figure out our values and morals, including those about sex. Some religions say that sex should be pleasurable, while others are shy about it! Some religions are accepting of sexual and gender diversity while others are really uptight about it. Fortunately, while in the UK & Ireland people have the right to practise whatever religion they choose, a religion cannot legally dictate what they can or cannot do. So, for example, even if a religion doesn't approve of sex before marriage, the person who does it cannot be legally punished.

Individual faith is a positive thing. Organised religion has a 'mob mentality' that's moralising and tells you what you can and can't do. I was quite religious growing up, and people in the church made me feel completely disempowered. I've had to navigate my own sexual landscape in the past year or so, re-educate myself. I still get flashes of guilt. *Dominique, 17*

Even so, it can be confusing or downright distressing for some teens who have grown up with religious teachings that make them feel there's something wrong with who they are.

I loved going to church when I was a teenager. I also knew I was gay. I resolved my relationship with God through therapy. My therapist taught me 'counter-theology' – questions like, 'What does your God want of you?' *Bee, from the podcast* **One Foot In**

I don't understand why (society thinks) violence that's everywhere in movies is OK, but we can't talk about periods and sex. We shield children from natural, healthy, pleasurable things, but not violence. I think (these attitudes) partly come from religion. *Holly, 24*

I want to talk to my kids about sex; my own mother never talked to me (about it). I've told my son, 'You have hormones, it's 100 per cent normal to feel attraction.' He learns at school that sex is OK. I've said to him, 'According to our religion, we have to control our desire. Sex before marriage is forbidden.' So I ask him to please talk to me as he gets older. *Nuzhat, mother of two teens*

Ethnic culture

My dad was Malaysian-Chinese and my mum is Anglo-Australian. They had different language, cultural and religious backgrounds. I grew up bathed in rich and diverse languages, foods and festivals. When it came to teens and sex, both my parents were on the same page: girls had to 'be good' and boys were just boys. My fight for gender equality started then and there. *Dr Melissa*

Everyone has a 'culture'. It's about the totality of you. Culture is a combination of your ethnic or racial heritage, your ancestry, traditions, languages, family and social systems, foods, beliefs and values. Some parts of your cultural identity might change over time. Ethnic culture is about the customs and beliefs that come from belonging to a particular racial or ethnic group. Some people, like us (Dr Melissa and Yumi), come from more than one ethnic background!

Ethnic cultures come with expectations about things like how we dress, how we treat family, going out with friends, dating, curfews and whether our gender should influence our behaviour. These all filter down into messages you'll hear about sex from the ethnic groups you belong to. Sometimes these messages are similar to what you see in the media and the bigger world around you, and other times quite different.

I met up with 'Mo' when I was 16, he was 17. We didn't have sex, we just talked. He said, 'Men like (you and me) will get married and cheat on our wives with men.' I didn't want that, I would never want that. I think that reflects attitudes towards women that are prevalent in Arabic culture; I think it denigrates women. *Bee, from the podcast One Foot In*

I feel like I have a cultural identity crisis. I am Korean and I have very Western friends. I'm very tied to my culture: I speak the language, I watch Korean movies, I have Korean friends. With my Western friends, sex is more commonly talked about, they're quite free, there's less judgement. And although Asians are seen as more introverted, I don't think that. We are all humans at the end of the day. *Jane, 22*

Parents and carers

Even if you tell yourself 'I don't care what my parents think about sex', chances are they've already been a huge influence on how you view it. Parents make the rules about behaviour, set boundaries and teach their kids social skills and life skills. They role-model and set the tone for A LOT – how much shyness or shame you feel about your body, how freely you can speak about emotions, love and confusing feelings. So it's no surprise if you find that your knowledge and attitudes about sex have come mostly from your parents/carers. Our hope is that you can talk to your parents, ask questions and add your parents to your trusted list of sources for info on sex.

Casual dating is something that goes on a lot around our age. But it's secretive casual dating, you know, going to the mall or something like that, away from parents. I don't think parents understand the way that they are keeping their child hidden from (sex) is bringing them closer towards it. *Sahib, 15*

My parents were very progressive and open-minded. My mum is Aboriginal and Dad is white. I asked at the dinner table when I was seven or eight years old, 'Where do babies come from?' and my dad gave a real detailed explanation of how sex works. Probably too much information! My older cousins were having kids quite young so when I was 10, my mum started to have conversations with me about sex, skewed towards pregnancy and risky elements. I thought, 'That won't be me – I've got other plans.' *Rudi Bremer*

When kids are learning and they get information wrong, parents or teachers will correct it and it's not taboo. But when they get information about sex wrong, it's not corrected – it's seen as funny or cute. Kids can later feel duped. *Professor Kerry Robinson*

I don't have a different attitude between my son and daughter. I don't think it should be different. I want to emphasise 'be valued, you don't need validation from others'. I don't want my son to have sex just to have a notch on his belt. *Christian, father of two sons*

91

Friends

Research all over the world tells us that teens are most likely to turn to their friends for information about sex. It's never as formal as, 'Hey, this is what I've learned recently!' – it's more like chatting about what you're doing, what you've heard others are doing, and what you wish you could do with Sexy McHottie over there!

Teens also learn about sex from broader social networks – like the kids in the rest of your class, your year, or your online social networks. No matter how original or independent we THINK we are, the research shows that we're very likely to make decisions about sex based on what our peers are doing.

I had an odd experience. I had a bet made against me and another mate about who would kiss first. It was at the end of Year 11 and neither of us had kissed anyone. All our mates, about 15 of them, had put a dollar on. Eventually the whole year knew about it. It sucked. *Seb. 19*

My friends don't talk about sex. One friend has Down's syndrome, they talk about sex and think it's more of a joke. I think sex should be talked about in private, not out in public. I should say if you want to talk about sexual references, do it in a place where no-one is uncomfortable. If people don't want to talk about it, don't make them go there. If your friend doesn't want to do that, don't make them. *Billy. 21. with autism and intellectual disability*

Someone in high school had heard the rumour that my first girlfriend and I had slept together. He came up to me and gave me a high five out of the blue, and then looked her up and down and shook his head in disgust and walked away! *Declan. 19*

School and teachers

Most teenagers say that school sex ed is NOT GOOD ENOUGH. They **want** to learn more at school about sex, consent and pleasure, sexual diversity, communication with an intimate partner and the actual mechanics of sex. (That's why we've devoted a lot of this book to these topics!) But school teachings about sex are often timid and inadequate because of a wider fear of saying the wrong thing, offending parents/carers, or going against the school's conservative history (which sometimes includes religion).

School sex ed was really bad! It didn't prepare me for anything I've experienced. It's also really sexist! There's so much on males. It made sex sound like something that was really invasive. It was like, 'This is what a man will do to you.' It was not explored with a sense of reality. And it was all about sex being a reproductive function: about sperm and pregnancy. They got us to repeat anatomical things and it didn't make any sense.

Year Eight was the most recent sex ed we had and we learned about how relationships work – which is this: couples go from holding hands to hugging, kissing, and then you massage them (!), and then you have sex. No oral. I had never heard of oral until the internet! I came across it and was like, 'WHAT THE HELL IS THAT.'

Consent was like a YouTube video they chucked on and not a word about pleasure. I didn't even know sex was FOR pleasure. I just thought it was a reproductive thing. *Ramona, 17*

Teaching about sexual diversity is more common in sex ed now compared to years ago. In my research I've seen some fantastic sex ed teachers. *Georgia Carr, sex ed researcher*

In Year Seven (sex ed) the boys and girls would split up and I remember one of my friends asked one of the teachers a question about something that wasn't relevant to the girls' end of the side, but more of the guys', and the teacher brushed it off. So it's like we just get taught about pregnancy and babies and hormones if we're a girl, but we don't get told about the other end – we only hear half the story, half of the conversation. *Sahib, 15*

I don't remember learning about body changes at school. I'm pretty much clueless – sometimes I search on the internet. My parents bought me two books but I didn't really read them! *Tom, 17*

Even if many people feel like their school sex-ed wasn't enough, it's still the one place kids hear about sex in an honest and scientific way. Years later, we still remember those lessons. It can be really important! Whether you're the kid who studiously pays attention or the one who stares out the window waiting for the bell, you're still absorbing messages about sex and sexuality. It might be directly from those incomplete sex ed or PDHPE classes, or from other subjects like religion and science. Teachers can be important role models, and it's not just what they teach, but how they react to real-life sexual behaviour that gets noticed by students.

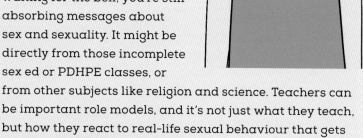

If you see school staff being disapproving about hickies or teen pregnancy, or not taking sexual harassment in the classroom seriously, this says that they aren't really up for open and honest communication about sex. And that can impact your trust in them and how YOU feel about sex, and talking about sex.

Health professionals

I've found with doctors there's a limitation with learning about sex. They talk about contraception, they ask you 'are you sexually active', they do STI tests. That's as far as it goes. There's no 'Sex 101' course that doctors provide. *Dominique, 17*

Health professionals often give messages to teens about sexual health. Government media campaigns sometimes try to do the same thing – but instead of telling you to wear a mask and wash your hands, they might tell you to wear a condom. A lot of the messages from health professionals are about sex being risky or dangerous to your physical health. That's because their jobs involve managing illness and preventing sickness, so they tend to focus on all the things that can go wrong, not all the things that can be great!

Media and social media

Everyone was quite sheltered around me. I think (that) was when I started exploring social media more (because) I felt like I was missing out on, you know, LIFE. I wasn't as developed because I didn't know things I wanted to find out about, and, yeah, I rushed into a lot of things. *Lisa, 23*

The media does this thing called stereotyping. It creates an idea and repeats it, as though it's the ONLY idea that matters. For example, a stereotype about sex might be that only certain body types are hot. Or that only thin, able-bodied people have sex. This isn't true – but it starts to FEEL true if you see it over and over again. And if you don't fit that stereotype, it can make you feel – falsely – as though you're not worthy of having enjoyable sex.

Another common stereotype is that only heterosexual sex is 'normal' – between a woman and a man. And also, that the woman is physically smaller, weaker and submissive while the man is bigger, stronger and in control. Stereotypes are dangerous because they don't tell the whole story – and usually they don't even tell the truth!

The truth is, all body types of all abilities can be – and feel – beautiful and sexy. Women are not weaker or submissive. Men don't have to be in control. People of all genders and sexualities and physicalities are totally, completely normal, and they can all be attractive. And everyone has the right to pleasure.

The media has a really big role in that they try to portray women as 'below' and men as 'superior'. You see it in movies and stuff; it's almost like the man has complete power. It's not right, but it's portrayed on TikTok, Instagram, Netflix – it's everywhere. *Sahib, 15*

There's some positives in the media. In the Elton John movie (*Rocketman*) there was a gay sex scene. It was a nice moment, done so tastefully. It's really important to present same-sex (sex and relationships) and diversity in positive ways. *Holly, 24*

Porn

Porn is videos or pictures of people having sex. It's designed to make the people watching it feel horny. There's nothing wrong with feeling horny, but porn can be the WORST teacher when it comes to sexual pleasure. Here's why.

It's all fake!

We all know that porn is fake, but it can still mess with our expectations about bodies, sex and pleasure. In real life, sex can be awkward, funny, silly and sweet – and you rarely see any of that in porn! Sex scenes very often completely ignore consent and protection, such as using condoms and checking in. The people in sex scenes are actors pretending to have sex, or pretending to enjoy having sex. The actors in porn are working hard to look good while they're doing it. Looking good is not your job when you're doing it IRL!

(Porn) made me feel really scared, like, 'Oh, I ain't as attractive as these women.' But I guess my view of porn is that it's not sex. They shouldn't be compared. It's all staged, and I just happen to get a sort of 'feeling' from it. Whereas sex is a lot more personal and explorative. And it releases those endorphins. Porn is just a quick sort of dopamine hit. *Lisa, 23*

I would say to young people – porn is like other kinds of entertainment, it's a kind of stunt. You know people do extreme stunts in movies, and in porn they do them with body parts. *Professor Kath Albury*

There's a lot about 'performance' in porn. I say to other young people, 'Porn is like a superhero movie. You're not going to have superpowers by watching it.' *Jessie, 23*

Concerningly, research tells us that young people are learning how to 'do' sex from porn … and they're often forgetting that their own pleasure is more important than how they 'perform'.

'Good porn' would reflect the diversity of people out there – different bodies, different ethnicities. A lot of the porn that young people see is degrading, especially towards women. It also depicts racial stereotypes. These days, porn is the most concentrated version of misogyny and gender inequality in popular culture. *Maree Crabbe, Director of It's Time We Talked (violence prevention program)*

Porn really misses the softness, patience and communication that people actually need and enjoy in real life. They're rarely depicted. If you never see people in porn using techniques that genuinely pleasure a clitoris, for example, how will you know how to do it?

Crappy stereotypes

A lot of porn amplifies stereotypes that are just plain wrong, such as that women don't have pubic hair and men have extra-large penises. In heterosexual porn, men are often shown as being dominating and aggressive. They might be slapping, choking or pulling the hair of the women they're having sex with.

To be very clear about this: these actions are 'niche'. They are **not** mainstream. They're not for everyone and not even for most people. To be slapped or choked or to have your hair pulled without a clear and explicit conversation about it beforehand is **assault**. Porn has normalised this behaviour for people, which is dangerous when translated into real-world sex. And for a lot of us, it's a huge turn-off. (Read more about consent in our book *Welcome to Consent*.)

Young men watching porn are likely to be masturbating to gendered inequality and aggression. Women in porn look like they love 'what the men are doing to them'. It's deeply problematic. Young women are more likely to find it degrading and violent towards women. *Maree Crabbe, Director of It's Time We Talked (violence prevention program)*

My friend went home with this guy and he choked her the first time they had sex! It totally upset her and the vibe was killed. Dead. Why would he think it's OK to do that? *Angie, 43*

There are stereotypes in gay and lesbian porn as well. In gay porn, one man (the 'top') is dominating and can be aggressive while the other (the 'bottom') is shown as weak and submissive. A lot of mainstream 'lesbian porn' shows women having sex with each other, but it's usually made for men to watch – so it's all about show, and their techniques aren't real, sensitive or sexy.

It's very unrealistic. I've seen a lot of young men who have erection problems because of too much porn; it becomes a vicious cycle. *Dr Eva Jackson, sexual health physician*

The virginity myth

The whole 'virginity thing' – 'Am I? Aren't I?'
I think virginity is such an outdated and rigid
concept. People who think virginity makes
you a loser – that's so sad. Everyone is at
different points in their journey. Some people
are asexual. Some want to wait, maybe until
marriage. I think 'virginity' must be deeply
rooted in wanting to oppress women.
Dominique, 17

The word 'virginity' should be erased from the sex
dictionary! It's confusing and plays into a huge double
standard that discriminates against girls and women.

The most common 'definition' of virginity is when
someone has not had penis-in-vagina sex. Clearly this
meaning doesn't apply to people who are gay or lesbian,
who might never officially 'lose their virginity', no matter
how sexually experienced they are! So we reject it.

Virginity is a very flexible concept. It's not really
about what sexual act counts or doesn't count
– but about what you want it to mean. 'Virgin'
is ONLY ever a loaded term. It's never a value-
neutral term. It's a compliment or an insult. The
problem is not how you define it, but how
everyone else tries to define it for you.
Georgia Carr, sex ed researcher

Say you are a virgin and you have sex with another female for the first time, would you still be a virgin? I have asked around but I never got a straight answer. In my eyes, sex with another female is just like masturbation, so if the answer is 'you are not a virgin', technically you could lose your virginity to yourself. *Anonymous*

Virginity is given very unequal treatment between genders. It's often been considered more important for girls and women to remain 'virgins' before marriage than for boys or men. This attitude can be so extreme that in some cultures, girls are sent to a doctor or a midwife for a 'virginity test', which means her genitals are inspected to look at her hymen.

MORE ON p. 39

There are still traditions practised today where a bride has to show someone (such as her father or her husband's family) the bedsheets after her wedding night, to prove that she bled when her hymen was 'broken'. Boys and men are not subjected to these sorts of virginity tests.

I've talked a LOT with my friends about sex and not a single person bled the first time they had (PIV) sex. Not one. Unless they were also on their period. *Yumi*

The virginity myth also leaves a lot of teens wondering whether they have 'lost their virginity' because they use tampons, or they have masturbated and put their fingers or an object inside their vagina.

If a person has been sexually assaulted, they might also wonder if they have 'lost' their virginity. It's very much up to each person to decide how they answer that question – and it might change over time.

Surviving childhood sexual abuse has had such a big influence on my adult sex life. If I thought about it really deeply, the first time I had *consensual* sex, it would be high school, Year 10. I had a girlfriend and that was very, very sexual … we had a lot of sex at school, in the lunch breaks, up at her mum's house, at my house on weekends when we had sleepovers. *Alex-Rose, 50*

Having penis-in-vagina sex for the first time can be important and special. But it doesn't change the state of you. The first time you have a cup of tea, or eat solid food, doesn't change WHO YOU ARE. This idea of going from 'virgin' to 'not a virgin' by doing one act is bullshit. And it's used to control women. *Aileen Barratt, Author of Tinder Translator*

THIS IS WHY WE WANT TO SCRAP THE WORD 'VIRGINITY' - IT'S STUPID, JUDGEY, AND OUT-OF-DATE! IT MAKES MUCH MORE SENSE TO JUST DESCRIBE WHAT YOU HAVE OR HAVEN'T DONE - 'I'VE NEVER HAD PENETRATIVE SEX' OR 'I HAVEN'T HAD CONSENSUAL SEX', FOR EXAMPLE - **IF YOU WANT TO.**

MYTHS ABOUT SEX

Everyone else is doing it

WRONG!

You might know stuff about what your BFFs and close friends are doing. But can you guess how many kids in your class or year group have had sex? Research has shown over and over again that teens think 'everyone else is doing it', but the stats tell a different story. In Australia, by the time teens finish high school, on average around **half** have had penis-in-vagina sex, one fifth have NOT pashed another person, and around half have tried oral sex.

There's only one way to orgasm

WRONG!

Whatever your genital parts, reaching an orgasm can happen in different ways at different times, on your own or with another person. There is no 'ideal' way to have an orgasm. Another myth about orgasms is that they are an essential part of sexual pleasure. Not only can a person experience extreme sexual pleasure without having an orgasm, but sometimes people have an orgasm without feeling pleasure.

MORE ON p. 68

Long-lasting sex is 'good' sex

NOT ALWAYS

The only definition of 'good sex' is sex that is consensual and satisfying for the people involved. Feeling satisfied is a physical AND emotional state, regardless of whether it's a casual encounter or with a long-term partner. Sex is much more likely to be good when each person is able to communicate what they like and don't like. That can be about giving and receiving pleasure as well as aftercare.

MORE ON p. 176

You can't leave your partner with blue balls

WRONG!

When someone with testicles (balls) and a penis gets turned on, blood flows into the genital area. That's what gives them an erection and makes the testicles and scrotum swell. This usually creates pleasurable sensations, which build up in intensity. The intensity ends when the arousal dies down and blood flows back out of the area. This might happen after an orgasm. Arousal can also finish for other reasons, like being distracted, interrupted or just changing your mind.

If blood does keep flowing in, it builds up blood pressure in the penis and testicles. If the pressure remains high for a while, then what feels good can turn into discomfort, an ache or even pain around the testicles and up towards the groin. (By the way, there's no definition of what 'a while' means.) Some people notice a bluish tinge to the scrotum, hence the expression 'blue balls'. This same process can happen for people with a vulva (some people call it 'blue vulva' or 'blue flaps').

This myth has been used by men to put pressure on (usually) girls and women to have sex with them.

THE 'BLUE BALLS MYTH' IS THAT IF SOMEONE ELSE TURNS THE BALL-OWNER ON, IT'S THEN THEIR RESPONSIBILITY TO BRING THEM TO A CLIMAX - AND FAILURE TO DO SO WILL SOMEHOW DAMAGE THE BALLS!

It can also be a way to guilt-trip a partner who doesn't want to do particular sexual things. It sucks. If someone is really experiencing a build-up of pressure in their balls and wants relief, they could whisk themselves off to somewhere private and masturbate. Problem solved!

Blue balls are not enough to complain about – there's definitely a dull ache, but you can't really use that as an excuse for pressuring someone into making you finish. It's very tolerable pain! *Josh, 17*

Size matters

WRONG

The 'size matters myth' is that a larger penis equals a man being more 'manly', better at sex and just generally more sexy. This seems to be very much a male hang-up, since heterosexual women don't care all that much. But, hey, we get that plenty of penis-owners *really* worry about it.

I remember in Year Eight, there was a period when all the boys were measuring their penis length! I measured my penis. Then last year I went to a party and drank six beers and thought, 'I wonder how big it is now?' And I got home and measured it and was like, 'Wow! I always thought it was the same size since Year Eight!' I'm 19 and it's still growing. *Declan, 19*

Penises grow heaps during puberty and can double or even triple in size when they're erect. Try to remember that living in a size-obsessed world doesn't mean you have to become obsessed too. And if you're wondering about whether you have the right 'tools' to have sex with someone else, remember you'll be better at it if you focus on *their* pleasure zones. There's SO MUCH more to giving sexual pleasure than how big your penis is.

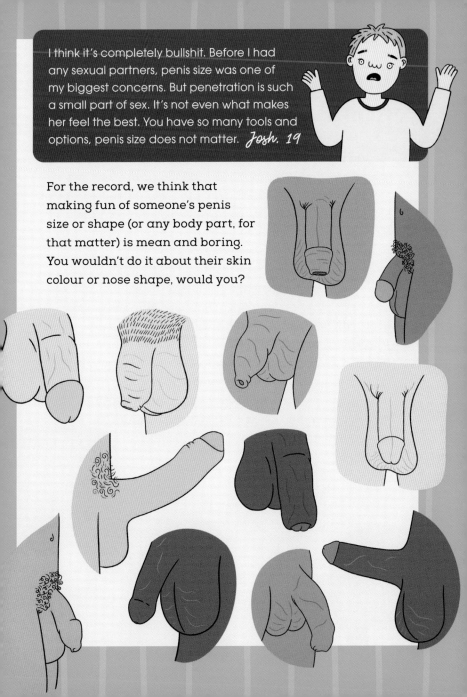

I think it's completely bullshit. Before I had any sexual partners, penis size was one of my biggest concerns. But penetration is such a small part of sex. It's not even what makes her feel the best. You have so many tools and options, penis size does not matter. *Josh, 19*

For the record, we think that making fun of someone's penis size or shape (or any body part, for that matter) is mean and boring. You wouldn't do it about their skin colour or nose shape, would you?

Vulvas have to be hairless to be sexy

WRONG!

It's sad to see how much we are taught to pick faults in our glorious bodies! Our 'imperfect' bodies aren't the reason we're not enjoying sex – they're the essential ingredient for sexual enjoyment! Embracing and accepting our bodies is a great start to loosening up and having fun when we're naked with another person.

Pubes are one of those elements of the human body that people can waste time agonising over.

They're there to help trap moisture from the genital area, which then gives off a sexy smell called a pheromone. And when two people with pubes grind on each other (having, for instance, penetrative penis-in-vagina sex), the pubes act as a 'dry lubricant', working together to create less friction and keep the skin underneath protected. Sounds like a good reason to hang on to at least some of those pubes, hey?!

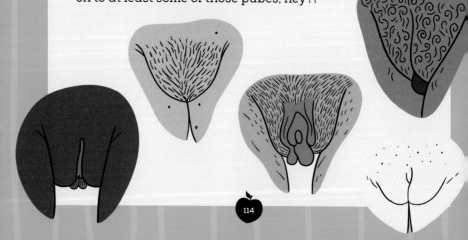

I felt pressured in school when all my friends were waxing off their pubes and I felt like I had to do the same thing! But I have this birthmark on my pubis and I was so embarrassed because the pubes used to hide it. So I ordered this REMOVE YOUR OWN BIRTHMARK kit from the internet. And it came with this cream and this emery board and you were meant to put the cream on and then chafe it with the emery board and then it would scab off! Of course the birthmark grew back. So did my pubes! *Gemma*

Pube fashion changes over time and in different cultures. Some want a trendy trim, others want them all gone, others are all up for the full bush.

Having fun with pube hairdos should be about what you want, and to your taste, not anyone else's. It's totally fine to leave them alone and enjoy your fluffy tufts as much as you want.

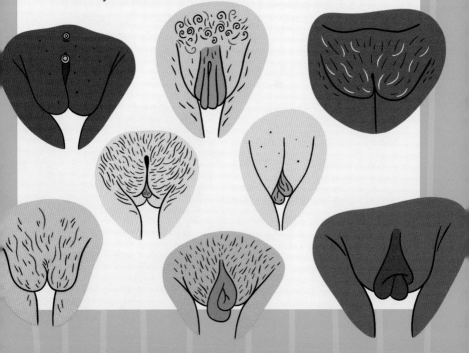

REASONS TO NOT HAVE SEX

Regardless of what the outside world is telling you about sex, there could be some really good reasons NOT to do it right now.

You're not ready

66 I went out with my boyfriend on the weekend and he leaned over to kiss me ... and I rejected him. I guess I was full of nerves. Sometimes I wonder if I'll ever get to kiss a guy ... am I just a really shy person? Or am I just not ready for it? **99**

Not being ready is an excellent reason NOT to have sex! Research tells us that teens who haven't had sex *because* they aren't ready feel really good about their decision. Being confident about what you *don't* want is super mature.

I'm less experienced than the average 19-year-old. I'm not super sexually active. It's not something that I feel any need to rush, and I find it hard to try to have sex with anybody I don't really feel comfortable with or know well. Casual hook-ups are not on the table for me. *Cara, 19*

I've had boyfriends, and there were times when I was close to consenting (to intercourse) and taking that step further, but I didn't find assurance in those individuals. I want to make sure I make the right decisions. I think about the emotional and social consequences. *Jane, 22*

I have had a lot of young boys talk to me in private, regretting that they had sex too young, or they weren't ready and couldn't say no. *Jenny Walsh, sex education expert*

You're just not into it!

> I've done literally nothing. I've never been in a relationship. Never kissed anyone. *Charlotte, 17*

This is an excellent reason! Some people are not into sex some of the time and some are not into it at all. Other people become more interested as they get older, while others become less interested. You do you!

> The worst advice is to 'just get it over and done with'. That's not to say that your first experience has to be this ultimate experience, because 99 per cent of the time it's going to be awkward or pretty bad! But this 'just get it done' attitude leads people to uncomfortable situations, to false expectations of how sex should be. *Seb, 19*

> When we were putting the condom on the banana (in sex ed class) I was thinking, 'This is so bizarre. I won't be doing this for a long time.' It didn't relate to me in Year Eight! *Gladys*

It's illegal

There is a law called the 'age of consent'. This law says
that **until you reach a certain age**, it is illegal to have
certain types of sex: oral sex, penis-in-vagina sex, anal
sex, and fingers going in the vagina or anus. (See What
can actually happen with another person on page 137.)
The law is in place to protect teens from being abused by
older people – or people in positions of power, such as a
teacher, coach, police officer, religious instructor or foster
carer.

In the United Kingdom and Ireland, the age of consent
is 16 or 17, depending on which country you live in.
This means if you're **under this age** and a person who is
older has sex with you, they are breaking the law. BUT if
the age difference is small – less than two or three years,
depending on where you live – the law might take this
into account.

You're doing it for the wrong reasons

One of the most exciting things about growing up is learning to figure out what's right and wrong for YOU. When it comes to sex, sometimes it's straightforward: a definite 'yes, it feels right' or a definite 'no, it feels wrong'. But it's often more complicated!

Deciding what's right or wrong for you means asking yourself if you're ready. It ALSO means paying attention to the other person, checking in with what's right for them and understanding consent. And it's ALSO making sure you're not motivated by the **wrong** reasons.

Some of these reasons are:

- You're feeling pressured
- You're doing it because you want friends to think you're cool
- You're ticking off a checklist
- You're scared to say no
- You're hoping the sex will result in a relationship
- You're drunk, or they're drunk, or you're both drunk
- You're trying to hurt or get back at someone
- The person you want to have sex with is only doing it with you for one of the above reasons

A common thread here is a lack of respect, for either yourself or the other person. So, if there's a gut feeling you have, or a voice in your head whispering, 'Nah ...' then trust in that, and give it more time.

I did not have sex until I went to uni – but I lied and told my friends I had. Heaps of people at school lie about having sex when they're not.
Anonymous

You don't have STI or pregnancy prevention

If you're planning penis-in-vagina sex where pregnancy could happen, then ask yourself: *Am I OK with becoming/ making this person pregnant?* Condoms prevent pregnancy and STIs, and are safe and readily, legally available for all ages. No-one will care if you're the one buying them. We promise!

MORE ON p. 221

If you do have penis-in-vagina sex without using birth control, or your first method fails in the moment (like the condom breaks), then there's also an effective 'emergency pill' that can be taken afterwards.

You're scared

“ I've been going out with my boyfriend for a while now and he asked me if he could finger me. I think I'm ready but I'm scared that I'll be too tight or he will judge me. Will it hurt me? **”**

“ Me and my boyfriend are ready to have sex but I'm scared it will hurt when I break my hymen. I've tried to use tampons and I can't, so what if his penis doesn't fit? **”**

We all know what it's like to feel nervous or scared about doing something we haven't done before. But there's a difference between excited nervousness and actually feeling afraid.

Many teenagers worry that when a finger or penis goes inside their vagina, it will hurt. The short answer to this fear is that if you're horny and ready for it, it should never hurt. And

if it does? Slow down.

Those with a penis can also be afraid sex will hurt them, too – the penis and testicles are very sensitive! Others are worried about being judged or laughed at for not 'doing it right' or being a bit clueless. It could be fear of pregnancy or STIs, or fear of getting busted by your mum. It can feel like a lot is at stake – worrying how others will

MORE ON p. 260

see you, gossip, failure, the impact this new thing might have on your relationship, or how you might end up feeling about yourself.

This can be especially hard for teens who want to have sex with someone of the same gender and worry about their own emotional or physical safety. If you're scared to have sex because it's not 'straight' sex and this could be a big deal in your family or community, or for you personally, there are ways to get support and advice.

MORE ON p. 283

SEX IS PLEASURABLE – IF IT HURTS, IT'S NOT HAPPENING RIGHT. EVEN THE FIRST TIME!

There's nobody around to have sex with

> **Everyone these days is having sex and (they) all have boyfriends but me. I feel I am ready to have sex and be in a relationship ... I am 15 but no guy seems to want to go out or have sex with me. PLEASE HELP!!**

Wishing for a romantic or intimate relationship – or wanting to just *have sex!* – comes with being human. But finding someone who wants to have sex with you, and who you want to have sex with, is tricky! At school there are always people who seem to find partners with amazing ease. And others who seem perpetually single, even though they crave connection!

If you can't have sex because you can't find a partner, first up – you're not the only one. Statistically, more people leave school having NOT had sex than having had it.

Second? Don't wait to be asked. Maybe you need to make the first move!

Third, there's no rush. Honestly. Not having sex does NOT mean there's something wrong with you. And you've got DECADES to find someone, or for someone to find you. Don't panic!

I was desperate to have sex and hook up in high school – but I was hopeless at it! Hopeless! I couldn't even find someone to take to my formal. I think it was because I was kind of a misfit and awkward and angry! As soon as I left school I found other dorks who were more like 'my people' and it got better. *Yumi*

How do I know if I'm ready?

We hear this question a lot from teens. Figuring it out can mess with your head! There's no one way to know if you're ready, but some questions you can ask yourself are:

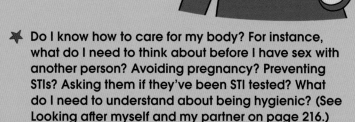

🌟 Do I know how to care for my body? For instance, what do I need to think about before I have sex with another person? Avoiding pregnancy? Preventing STIs? Asking them if they've been STI tested? What do I need to understand about being hygienic? (See Looking after myself and my partner on page 216.)

⭐ Do I understand that nervousness and excitement might be overwhelming and that I don't have to go through with it?

⭐ What are the reasons I DO want to have sex? Are the reasons about me – or about the other person?

🌟 Will I be able to say what I like and don't like, and be listened to? (Um … do I even know what I like and don't like?)

🌟 Will I feel safe?

126

★ How confident am I that I will respect myself, and be respected, even if things feel awkward or don't quite go to plan? (See Wobbly starts on page 178 and Respectful relationships on page 212.)

★ Will I be able to call 'stop' if I want to? And be listened to?

★ Does the idea of doing it make me feel excited, or sick and terrified?

★ Is there something different that we could be doing that I'd prefer to do?

★ Am I giving consent freely? Is the person I want to have sex with giving consent freely? (See Consent, sex and pleasure on page 141.)

Consent means you, and the other person, agree to have sex – equally and mutually. If one doesn't want to, it could be for any of the reasons above, and that's OK. Saying 'no' or 'I'm not ready' shows maturity and doesn't mean there isn't an attraction or the other person isn't worthy.

HOW IT BEGINS: FEELINGS, FLIRTING AND FALLING IN LOVE

Sometimes when you're on the wild roller-coaster ride that is puberty, it's good to slow down and just *feel*. Connecting with another person always begins with feeling *something*. Those feelings can be intensely distracting, crushingly sad or magically happy. They can be Big Feelings or small feelings. From crushes to sexual attraction to falling in love, getting to know your feelings is as important as getting to know your body ... you can't really separate them.

5

4

3

2

1

> We weren't told anything at school about the emotional aspects of sex. It's like they think people don't experience any feelings when they have sex with someone! *Natalie, 28*

Sex is emotional as well as physical. In my research we've found that young men don't always have the vocabulary about feelings. We've developed a web resource called *Crushed But OK* for young men to help them understand their feelings in relationships. Young people use emojis to convey a lot of emotions, but they can be confusing. *Professor Kath Albury*

I have spoken to thousands of men about sex and pleasure and I believe that men are actually more emotional about sex than women are. *Jacqueline Hellyer, sex therapist*

Attraction

Attraction is a feeling of intense *like* towards, or interest in, someone else. That feeling might be deep and long-lasting, or it might be short-lived. We can be attracted to people of any gender, and that can change over time.

QUESTIONS FOR DR MELISSA

66 I'm 17 (and male) and I really like girls, but I keep having dreams that I'm kissing my (male) friends. I don't want to be gay but I think I could be if my dreams don't stop. Please help me stop the dreams. 99

66 I'm a 14-year-old girl and dream of having sex with girls (but I have a boyfriend). Does this mean I am bisexual or a lesbian or just normal? 99

Many teens have asked what it means if they feel a romantic or sexual attraction to people of the same gender. Sometimes dreams have confused them, other times it was feeling attraction when wide awake. Try not to get too hung up on what it means to have a dream, fantasy or desire – your body is rewiring and your hormones are going bananas on account of this puberty business! It doesn't mean that what you're feeling isn't real, just that you're going through some extra-hectic turbulence at the moment.

Having a crush

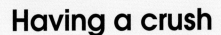

When you have a crush on someone, you think about them a LOT and your heart races when they look at you or brush past you. Things seems boring when they're not there, and you feel sick when you think about them kissing someone else!

Crushes are about emotional experiences AND physical ones. It's A LOT! Having a crush on someone might be your first experience of what romantic infatuation feels like. A lot of us get crushes on someone we're never likely to meet, like a celebrity or famous athlete. Or it could be someone from real life, but who would never consider us as a partner! We tend to idealise the person we're crushing on – we consider them to be EXTRA wonderful, amazing, clever and attractive, even when, realistically, no-one is perfect.

Having a crush on someone doesn't mean you will, or even that you want to, have sex with them. But it's part of growing up: crushes are like a practice go at love!

Sexual attraction

Sexual attraction, or 'having the hots' for someone, is a new experience for many teens. It's different from a crush (although the two things can overlap) because there are tingly or just plain HOT feelings that are intensely physical. The desire to 'get physical' can be much stronger than wanting to just vibe with someone who's smart, or funny, or kind.

Having the hots is more of a lustful way of thinking about someone; having a crush is more emotional, but they're pretty interchangeable.
Declan, 19

Your body reacts when they're around, and it can feel like heat is emanating from your undies! You might feel like you want to touch or BE touched by the person – often both. Sometimes sexual attraction can be so intense that it overtakes other feelings, such as romance, love or like, or even dislike.

SOME PEOPLE DON'T EXPERIENCE SEXUAL ATTRACTION UNTIL LATER ON IN LIFE, AND SOME DON'T AT ALL.

Sexual attraction and feelings

Even when sexual desire is intense, for most people, emotions still play a big part in pleasure and enjoyment. Sure, you might be thinking a LOT about having sex with a particular person, but your brain's emotional response to the person can change your sexual attraction dramatically. Someone you've just shared a deep, soul-shaking laugh with could be the person with whom you have an amazingly pleasurable sexual experience. But if they acted like a jerk, or you're not getting the same 'hot' vibes from them, or you've had a mild disagreement with them, it can dampen your desire.

TURN OFF TURN ON TURN OFF TURN ON TURN OFF TURN ON

Flirting

Flirting is a playful way of communicating with another person. It's meant to be fun. It can communicate to the other person that you're attracted to them, you like them, or you want their attention. It can have a sexual energy, but it doesn't necessarily mean you want to have sex with the other person, or that you're even thinking about sex!

QUESTIONS FOR DR MELISSA

" I'm 13 and I've had this 'thing' going on with a guy at my school. On the last day of school I started to act more interested in him and it kinda worked because (then) he started to follow me to all the same activities I'd choose and sit next to me and talk to me. We kinda flirted a little bit but then we had to leave for the school holidays and now IDK what to do once school starts. **"**

" I'm really confused, me and my crush flirt all the time but IDK if he likes me or is just being friendly. How do I know if he likes me or not? **"**

Because flirting sometimes happens when two people don't know each other very well, it can be sexy as hell but it can also create confusion and misunderstanding. Body language that's commonly used in flirting, like smiling,

Some disabled people will be the sexiest hornbags in the world! It's part of their self-expression to show everyone how amazingly HOT they are. Other disabled people will be a little quieter in their sexiness, and that's fine too. *Madeleine Stewart, 28, disabled comedian*

also happens when you're not flirting at all! Flirting happens online or in person and it's something people do whether they're young or old. Some people love flirting, and others aren't into it at all – and lots of people find it takes a bit of practice to feel comfortable flirting.

Fun fact: researchers have studied the way people flirt all over the world in different

countries and cultures. They have found that it nearly always involves smiling, making eye contact, laughing and imitating the other person.

Falling and being in love

Falling in love is real. It can happen in your teens or when you're 100, and it can be a powerful emotional ride! Falling in love triggers the release of a whole bunch of brain chemicals and hormones that can give us energy, make us lose our appetite, sleep less and feel exhilarated. The state of 'falling in love' is really energetic, but the brain chemicals involved settle down after somewhere between six months and a couple of years. (Brain scientists and psychologists believe this is because we would probably burn out!)

After that time, if you're still with the person you fell in love with, you might switch to 'being in love', which is less intense. Being in love involves feeling a deep connection or 'attachment' to someone – similar to how we feel towards close friends or family members, except that there's also an element of romance or sexual intimacy.

WHAT CAN ACTUALLY HAPPEN WITH ANOTHER PERSON?

Welcome to your L-plates

Learning about sex starts **long before** your teen years and continues throughout your life. Hopefully you will keep learning about sex well into old age!

By the time you're ready to have sex with another person, you will already have heard hundreds of messages about sex from the world around you. Maybe you and your partner will have formed ideas about what you are supposed to do from porn? Maybe you think that everyone else knows what to do (hint: they don't) and it'd be too embarrassing to admit you haven't done this before. Maybe gossip and chatter at school have laid out what's considered 'normal' – and you're not sure if you want that.

MORE ON p. 84

In this section we'll be talking in detail about getting physically intimate with another person. Remember that there's **no set menu** for what you should and shouldn't do with another person. Here are some basic guidelines to start with:

Get to know your own body first and what feels good for you! (See Getting intimate with myself on page 30.)

Figure out what you think you might like to do with another person.

Decide your boundaries – and consider how you and your partner can protect and respect your boundaries and theirs (see Consent, sex and pleasure on page 141).

Then think about how you're going to communicate, give and receive consent.

If you think you might do stuff that could lead to STIs or an (unplanned) pregnancy, get the equipment you'll need to prevent them! (See Contraception on page 220.)

And then try stuff out – and remember to check in with your partner regularly to see if they're feeling OK about what you're both doing.

I'm ready to ... know more about sex, intimacy and pleasure

In sex scenes on TV shows, you see them kissing and getting into it, then you see them at the end when 'it's' all over, and no-one tells you what happens in the middle!
Brenda, mother of two teens

A lot of the younger kids I know are watching porn and are watching it before they know anything else about sex. It's really important to know that porn is NOT educational and is not what real sex is like. And they need to know that they don't have to look like anyone in there. *Phoebe, 17*

There's not a 'right way' to 'do sex'.
Professor Deborah Bateson

In this part of the book, we've taken cues from the thousands of questions that Dr Melissa answered from teens about sex over many years.

QUESTIONS FOR DR MELISSA

66 I don't have a clue what orgasm, oral sex and intercourse are – please tell me. **99**

66 I'm 16 and am scared to have intimate relationships with guys because of various reasons. Firstly I don't know how to arouse guys, like how to give them blow jobs, hand jobs, what things to do in foreplay or even where to kiss, suck, rub or blow on any part of their body. I'm worried that they will laugh at me because I don't know how to do any of this. **99**

66 Should sex moments be happy or sad? **99**

Don't worry. We'll cover everything you want to know ... and sex moments can be happy, sad, hilarious, kind, profoundly meaningful or silly.

Consent, sex and pleasure

Consent means 'an agreement between people that they both want to do something'. We wrote a whole book about it, called *Welcome to Consent*. It applies in everyday situations in life, like agreeing to lend your friend a shirt! And it's SUPER important when it comes to physical touch, intimacy and sex.

What feels good for you might not feel good for someone else, and vice versa. And, just to confuse things, what feels good (or not) can and does change, day by day, or moment by moment. Whatever you're feeling, it is always your right to say *NO*.

> I'm 19 and definitely still learning about sex. It took me a long time to realise that it's supposed to feel good! It's supposed to feel enjoyable – it's not just the act for the sake of the act. *Izzy, 19*

You might not be sure whether **you want** to do something or not. That's very understandable. Especially if you've never done it before! So the essential ingredient for consent is enough time to figure out your feelings and what your gut instinct is telling you.

Consent is all about **respect** and **bodily autonomy**. Respect is knowing that your feelings and rights count – and so do other peoples'. Bodily autonomy means being the boss of your body. Even if you need help doing things with your body (such as a little kid needing help to get dressed, or someone with a disability who needs help mobilising), your body still belongs to you.

Consent is also more than asking, 'Do you want to have sex?' and the other person saying, 'Yes!' It's an ongoing conversation: 'Does this feel good? Do you want to stop?' You're both allowed to change your mind at any time. Each person has to regularly check in, and learn how to listen to *and* observe the other person's responses (remember, non-verbal cues such as shaking the head are just as important as someone saying 'No!' out loud).

You are always in charge of what you do and don't do when it comes to sex!

Touch

66 Our hands were near each other's and he moved his so I was holding his thumb. I'd squeeze it every now and then to let him know I knew. He then moved it so I was holding his pointer finger then so we were holding hands. I told a friend and she said I definitely like him (cause I don't know my own feelings) and another friend said he definitely likes me. What do I do?! 99

66 My ex and I are still pretty close and when he gave me a hug today I got a funny sensation in my vagina, kind of like a mini orgasm. Is this normal? And what is it? 99

66 I'm only 14 and feel that I sometimes have an urge to kiss girls or want girls, and I'm a girl. Does that mean I'm a lesbian? Sometimes I hug them or kiss them but they think it's friendship. I think it's love and horniness! 99

Getting intimate with another person often starts with everyday touch, like holding hands or hugging. But somehow it feels different – because it is! How you feel about that person makes your experience of touching them very different. Touching the hand of someone you're romantically attracted to can feel **electric**.

Hugs can mean love,

affection, friendship or caring. In some cultures, they're a form of greeting. But hugging someone you're romantically or sexually attracted to is different. It can trigger those pleasure hormones that make us feel sexually turned on, or just really, really happy.

When you're getting sexually intimate with someone for the first time, a close hug with them might leave you tingling. It's good to communicate that you want or like this touch, and to check if it feels nice for them too. You might say, 'That feels nice!' or 'Ooh, I didn't know that a hug could feel so good!' or maybe just, 'Mmmm!' You might convey that you're enjoying the touch by making eye contact, smiling or snuggling in.

A delightful picnic table laden with sexy options

When you're first starting out, some ways to have sex with another person might happen before others; for example, sexual kissing might happen before any kind of nudity or touching of another person's genitals. A lot of the time, sexual kissing and touching happens

before oral sex or intercourse. Sexting or sending nudes might come somewhere in the middle.

BUT you don't have to follow this script every time you have sex. In fact, you shouldn't! No one type of sex is the best, or the 'end game'. Switch it up, mix it up and ditch the hierarchy!

Picture instead a delightful picnic table, topped with a dazzling array of delicious and delightful options. Which one do you want to try first? Do you have a favourite? Is there something there you've never seen before? And what about that dish you can't stand? Yuck! Do you want to heap your plate high, or savour just one or two morsels?

The beauty and delight of having a table full of options is that you can pick and choose each time. You can choose according to what's suitable for your partner. If, for instance, they have a physical disability, sex while doing handstands may not be appropriate! You can pick according to your mood!

When I was a teen, I remember kids talked about 'bases' when it came to a timeline of sexual activity – first, second, third and home base. Today I sometimes hear people talk about 'levelling up'. I find this whole idea of ranking types of sex really messed up. Everyone should be free to figure out what they like and don't like, and how it changes, or not. The idea of having to fit into some old-fashioned hierarchy can make sex pretty boring and leaves out a lot of ways to have pleasure and fun. *Dr Melissa*

Here are some of the things you may find on the picnic table as an L-plater at this feast:

Sexual kissing

❝I am 14 and I've never pashed a guy. I'm worried that when I do I won't know how. I'm embarrassed to ask my friends, but I would like to know what you do with your tongue while pashing. Please help? Thanks! ❞

Sexual kissing is different from polite, affectionate or friendly kissing. A sexual kiss involves both people touching their lips, mouths and tongues together. Words for this include 'pash', 'snog', 'making out', 'French kiss', 'tongue kiss' and 'deep kiss', and it often involves your whole body pressing up against the other person. It's intimate.

Making out is meant to feel awesome – it switches on the pleasure hormones and leads to sexual arousal. The lips and mouth can easily become pleasure zones in the right circumstances! Sexual kissing can also be emotionally charged – some people find sexual kissing to be the **most intimate** of all sexual activities. Sexual kissing can be an important way of bonding people who are in a relationship.

While everyone's attention was on the movie we were giving each other little forehead kisses and cheek kisses, and then she kissed me on the mouth. And then we made excuses and went downstairs and made out for a while. At the time it felt like the best thing ever! I remember thinking, 'This is amazing!' *Tiger, 19*

I used to hate kissing. I used to think it was so embarrassing and gross! *Phoebe, 17*

The closeness, the connection, is nice, and there is just something within people that just enjoys kissing. If you're attracted to or in love with someone that definitely makes it better. If it's a random kiss on a dancefloor it's enjoyable, but doesn't have the other connections to it. *Declan, 19*

How do you kiss?

A lot of what makes kissing exciting is the way you tune in to the other person, respond to what they're doing and find harmony in what you do together. So, naturally, there's no right or wrong way to kiss! What you and your partner enjoy one time can change the next, and be completely different with a new partner.

This type of kissing might last a few seconds or several minutes. It might begin with each person touching their lips to the other's. The lips might be closed, or slightly open. Each person usually tilts their head so that each pair of lips can touch easily (fun fact: most people tilt their head to the right!). As the kiss progresses, each person opens their mouth a little wider and might put their tongue inside the other person's mouth. They might swirl their tongues around for a second or two, a little or a bit more. You might move to nuzzle the neck and jaw and behind the ear, which feels extra lovely. Each person might 'stop and start' the same sequence over and over. Some people open their mouths wide and others just a little.

148

Young people sometimes feel pressure to 'pash' someone. Some have said that the expectations they had about sexual kissing were so great that when it actually happened, it was hugely disappointing. In some cases, it killed the relationship they were in. So, hey, don't pressure other people (or yourself!) to kiss someone. It will happen when it happens! Others love to kiss and have found it bonding and sexy and super exciting. Most teens experience sexual kissing a few years before having other kinds of sex.

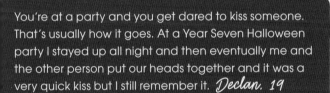

You're at a party and you get dared to kiss someone. That's usually how it goes. At a Year Seven Halloween party I stayed up all night and then eventually me and the other person put our heads together and it was a very quick kiss but I still remember it. *Declan, 19*

Should I ask before I kiss someone?

Yes! Like any intimate touch, it's important that each person consents to a kiss. You can then continue communicating about what feels good and what doesn't. Getting consent verbally is the gold standard, but non-verbal communication can work a lot of the time too.

You might say, 'Is this OK?' or, 'Hey, can I kiss you?' or, 'I really want to kiss you …?' Body language might imply consent if each person leans in towards the other, makes eye contact, kisses back or simply smiles and looks eager.

The best way to enjoy making out is to check in as you go. You or your partner might make noises that convey pleasure, such as, 'Mmmmm!', 'Ooohh!' or a happy or excited sigh. Or you might press your body closer to theirs, or run your hands over their back. Or you might not do any of that! It's up to you.

If you're not finding the mouth or tongue action pleasurable, you can pull back or stop and say:

Hang on a sec.

I just want to catch my breath.

That feels weird.

Can we pause?

TAKE NOTE OF WHAT YOUR PARTNER IS COMMUNICATING AS WELL. YOU CAN CHECK IN WITH THEM BY ASKING, 'YOU OK?' OR, 'DO YOU LIKE THIS?'

Sexual touching

Getting to know your erogenous zones by yourself (see Masturbation on page 52) is a great way to discover sexual pleasure. But it's quite different from doing it with someone else – like the way tickling yourself doesn't work! When you and a partner decide you want to touch each other, it should be pleasurable and satisfying for each of you. What you each feel like and enjoy one time could be different the next time. It's good to check in with each other!

> I spent so long tracing my fingers up and down their back. They say if you hug someone for 20 seconds your dopamine is released. Skin-on-skin is so valuable in making you feel truly alive and present. *Phoebe, 17*

Touch anywhere on the body can feel hot and sexy when you're turned on and into the other person. Those sensations often ramp up when a partner touches the more sensitive parts of your body, such as the legs, lower back, soft part of your arm, nipples, breasts, inner thighs and anywhere that's inside your undies. Some people also get turned on when other body parts are caressed – such as the neck, earlobes, inner-knees, feet or scalp!

It's not uncommon for teens to get into sexual kissing and then sexual touching. (These two things often happen at the same time.) Sexual touching can happen with clothes on – it can feel pleasurable to have your partner's hands moving, rubbing or brushing over your different erogenous zones.

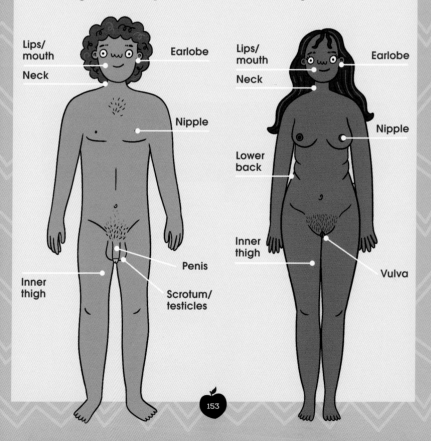

Lips/mouth
Earlobe
Neck
Nipple
Inner thigh
Penis
Scrotum/testicles

Lips/mouth
Earlobe
Neck
Nipple
Lower back
Inner thigh
Vulva

Fingering

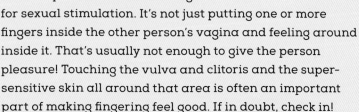

Fingering is when someone uses their hands and fingers to touch another person's vulva and vagina for sexual stimulation. It's not just putting one or more fingers inside the other person's vagina and feeling around inside it. That's usually not enough to give the person pleasure! Touching the vulva and clitoris and the super-sensitive skin all around that area is often an important part of making fingering feel good. If in doubt, check in!

Oh, and first step: **make sure hands and fingers are clean!**

> Teenage boys are no good at fingering! They jab at you. I don't think they really understand what they're doing. They're poking in and hoping for the best. *Ramona, 17*

Fingering should feel great! It's possible for many people to have an orgasm this way. But what feels great one time or with one partner can be quite different the next time. It should **never** feel painful or uncomfortable.

MORE ON p. 68

> I think most (straight) teenage boys understand that a vulva needs to be wet. Even if visually it isn't what you see in porn!
> *Seb, 19*

Wet is good

For fingering to feel pleasurable, having plenty of lubrication is important. When a vagina-owner is turned on (aka sexually aroused), the vagina naturally makes its own lubricant. It's a clear, watery liquid that seeps out of the vagina and onto the vulva, making the inside and outside nice and slippery.

If you can't feel any moisture, then they mightn't be as turned on as you. You may need to slow down and leave that area alone for a bit. You can also use some saliva (put some of your saliva onto your fingers before touching their vulva and vagina) or a small amount of bought lubricant.

> Girls can have sex in many different ways, using toys, fingers, mouths, grinding … The best part of girl-on-girl sex is that you don't need to worry about them finding your clit! There's a kind of softness to it. You feel a lot more safe. *Phoebe, 17*

How do you finger someone?

We can use our fingers in lots of creative ways when touching someone's vulva and vagina, vaginal opening and perineum. Fingers can rub, circle, gently squeeze or even give mini-massages. Moving them fast or slowly, changing the direction you move them in, and applying light or heavier pressure around the vulva and genital area are all ways to 'do' fingering. Starting as **gently** as possible is a smart approach – you can always apply more pressure later.

Putting one or more fingers inside the vagina can also feel very pleasurable for the vagina-owner. Usually you can tell if the time is right by checking for wetness. If their vagina is dry, they're **not** ready. How many fingers and how far inside to put them can vary – there are no rules, but check in with your partner and ask them what they like. Applying pressure to the inside vagina wall by gently thrusting the fingers in and out or pushing against the wall can also feel good.

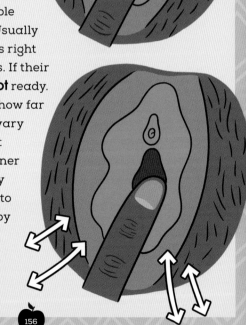

My tip would be – don't race to the vagina, or even the clitoris! There's so much delightful skin to be caressed on the vulva, the inner-inner-thighs, the bottom. If you can give this some attention before you 'dive in', the person you're with will really appreciate it! *Yumi*

I remember going to an under-age school dance in Year Eight and me and my friends were like, 'We're gonna get fingered tonight!' (It came true.) *Gemma*

Fingering can also mean using hands and fingers to touch someone's anus. (This is not for everyone, so **assume nothing!** Ask first.) Touching around it or putting a finger or two inside it can be very stimulating, but remember to wash your hands thoroughly afterwards before moving on to another body part (such as the vulva or vagina). The anus and the skin around it have bacteria around them that can easily find their way into the urethra and cause painful bladder infections. No jokes. This happens.

Wash those hands!

Hand jobs

> **I was recently talking to a friend and she said a guy fingered her and the guy wanted her to pull him off but she didn't know what to do. Until then, I thought I was the only one! Could you please explain what you have to do? It's really worrying me.**

A hand job, 'pulling someone off' or 'wanking them' means using your hands and fingers to touch someone else's penis. The penis might already be erect when you first touch it, or it might become erect while you do it. There are lots of ways to touch the penis – check with its owner and see what they like.

You might go from lightly brushing your fingers against the penis to wrapping your whole hand around the shaft of the penis (see page 56) and moving it up and down. Your partner might prefer being touched at the tip (glans) of the penis or having the entire penis and scrotum stroked.

It's nice having that intimate, physical bond (with hand jobs). And it's nice to have someone else who is willing to do that for you. *Josh, 17*

You can change the speed and the pressure you apply by asking your partner what feels good.

If your partner is not circumcised (see page 43), then it's likely that their foreskin will start to pull back as their penis gets fully erect. Some people enjoy having the foreskin gently played with, such as pulling it down or slipping a finger between the foreskin and the glans.

Lubrication also happens naturally when a penis-owner gets turned on. It's common for the penis to leak a bit of clear fluid (sometimes called 'pre-cum'), which makes the tip of the penis slippery. You can use some lube or saliva to help lubricate the whole penis (put some of your saliva on your fingers and hand). Again, ask your partner what feels good. Some people prefer a lot of lubrication, while others don't.

Oral sex

66 I want to know what a '69' is. My friends talk about it but I'm too embarrassed to tell them I don't know. 99

Oral sex means touching another person's genitals with the mouth, lips and tongue. The mouth and tongue are warm, soft and sensual, and produce their own lubricant (saliva) – so oral sex can feel really good! You might use your fingers as well. There are no 'right' or 'wrong' ways to have oral sex – it's about what you and your partner enjoy, and it might change each time.

Oral sex is better if you chat about it before you start! It's very intimate – not only is it about touch, but your sense of taste and smell can get more switched on, too.

A '69' is when two people are giving oral sex to each other at the same time. Their bodies are facing towards each other, and the position they're in together is like the number 69. Some people like it, some don't.

Oral sex on a vulva

A fancy word for this is called 'cunnilingus'; some slang words for it are 'going down on them', 'giving oral' and 'eating out'.

If you're wanting to pleasure a woman, read research written by women! They know themselves the best! And once you get into those situations – I have autism spectrum disorder so I need explicit communication – you can ask what they like and what feels good! *Seb. 19*

Giving oral sex to someone with a vulva can involve licking, sucking and stroking with the lips and tongue, or even the gentlest nibble-like biting. You can change the speed or pressure you use with your tongue and lips. Depending on what your partner wants, you can concentrate just on one area (such as licking the clitoris from side-to-side) or you can move around. The most sensitive parts of the vulva are the clitoris, the vaginal opening and the perineum. You can use your hands to touch the area as well. Check in with what your partner likes and doesn't like!

You might like to use dental dams during oral sex – see page 231.

Oral sex on a penis

"Confused! Are 'giving head' and 'blow job' the same thing? And what do you do to their penis? Do you blow into it, or just lick it? "

'Giving head,' 'sucking off' and 'blow jobs' all mean using the mouth and tongue to touch a person's penis and scrotum. A fancy word for this is 'fellatio'.

You can move your mouth and tongue up and down the penis, or put it in your mouth and move your mouth up and down on it. Your hands can get involved as well. If the penis touches the back of your throat, it can make you gag, so be careful! You can pause, adjust how far in their penis goes, or just stop.

Communicate beforehand about ejaculation. They should ask what you prefer. You can say you don't want them to ejaculate in your mouth and make sure you're able to pull your head away when they're about to come. Or, if you're OK with it, it's safe to swallow the semen. You can also spit it into a tissue or sink. Or you could get them to use a condom, see page 223.

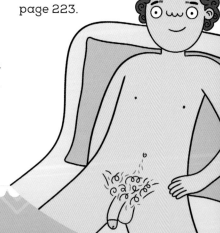

Intercourse

We're talking mostly about penis-in-vagina (PIV) sex or penis-in-anus ('anal') sex.

PIV sex involves putting an erect penis inside a vagina, moving it in and out for stimulation and friction, and often finishes with orgasm for the penis-owner.

Anal sex involves putting an erect penis inside an anus, moving it in and out for stimulation and friction, and often finishes with orgasm for the penis-owner.

Written like that, intercourse sounds pretty average! Ha! But lots of people quite like it.

Some people use sex toys in a similar way, putting them inside their partner's vagina or anus.

Important!

Of all the different ways to have sex, intercourse has the greatest risk of passing on a sexually transmitted infection if one person has an STI. (Fact: most young people with an STI have no symptoms, so they could pass it on without realising.) PIV sex could lead to pregnancy. If you or your partner don't want to risk these things, then check out Looking after myself and my partner on page 216 first.

Mutual pleasure

I didn't even realise sex was meant to be pleasurable. Only last year I understood that sex and pleasure were meant to be intertwined.
Ramona, 17

Intercourse can be slow and lingering. It does NOT have to be fast and furious. You can have intercourse while simultaneously touching, licking or kissing other sensitive parts of the body. People have intercourse in different positions: lying down, standing up, one person on top of the other, facing towards or away from each other. It varies!

To have PIV sex, both people need to be pretty turned on, so that the penis is erect and the vagina well lubricated. Getting turned on happens in lots of ways, like kissing and touching. You start with gentle pushing of the penis into the vagina, sometimes quite slowly but always checking throughout that it feels OK. The penis might need to go back out a few times before the vagina is comfortable taking it all the way in.

Once the penis is all the way inside the vagina, intercourse might continue with the penis-owner thrusting their hips, which moves the penis back and forth while inside. The penis-owner might have an orgasm this way, and ejaculate. This can feel very pleasurable for the vagina-owner too, as the erect penis will be rubbing against the clitoris from the inside. (See The internal clitoris on page 38.)

Most vagina-owners *won't* have an orgasm from PIV thrusting, though. Either person could use their fingers to rub the clitoris for maximum stimulation *during* intercourse, while the penis is thrusting inside the vagina. Some positions can help the clitoris tip get rubbed more directly by the pad of skin above the penis. Other positions might angle the penis so it pushes more against the front of the vagina, near the inside part of the clitoris. It can be fun figuring out what positions your bodies, arms and hands need to be in to make this happen!

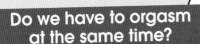

Do we have to orgasm at the same time?

No! Mutual pleasure *doesn't* mean simultaneous orgasms. It's not necessary – it can happen, but often doesn't.

It can actually be *more* pleasurable for everyone if the vagina-owner orgasms first, followed immediately by the penis going into the vagina. The contractions in the pelvic area (see Orgasms on page 64) can be felt around the penis and create extra stimulation for both.

Alternatively, the penis-owner could reach orgasm first, pull out their penis and then rub or lick the clitoris (or wherever feels good for the vagina-owner) until they orgasm.

A simultaneous, boy-girl orgasm has never happened to me, ever. Sometimes I come first, or sometimes I come after. Because I orgasm a lot on my own it's not the end of the world if I don't orgasm during partnered sex. *Gemma*

Scissoring

Scissoring is when two people intertwine their legs tightly so that their genitals touch, then rub together. It's not technically intercourse because nothing is going into a vagina or anus, but it can be just as stimulating.

The lowdown on anal sex

Everyone has an anus! It's located in a sensitive part of the body, so touching the skin around the anus can be a huge turn-on for people of any gender. You generally want to get started on this kind of sex play **after** a soapy shower, so that the area is extremely clean!

One person might gently tickle or lick the area (called 'rimming') around the anus before making contact with the actual skin of the butthole with their penis.

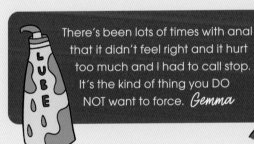

There's been lots of times with anal that it didn't feel right and it hurt too much and I had to call stop. It's the kind of thing you DO NOT want to force. *Gemma*

Compared to the vagina, the anus is not as stretchy and doesn't lubricate naturally – so sex here should pretty much **always** involve water-based lubrication. (Lube can be bought from supermarkets, convenience stores, chemists and servos. No-one cares when you buy it, seriously.) Without lube to make the anus slippery, penetration can be uncomfortable and even pretty painful.

When two penis-owners have anal sex, they might talk about being a 'top' or a 'bottom'. A top is the one whose penis goes inside the other person's anus and a bottom is the one who 'receives' the other person's penis. Contrary to popular opinion, having anal sex isn't necessarily on the menu in guy-on-guy sex.

The people I've been sexual with, if you're cuddling and having sex talk, when I ask, 'What's off-limits for you?' most of them say anal. *Seb. 19*

No-one has to do anal if they don't want to. Most teens don't! Because of the tightness of the anus, the lack of naturally occurring lubrication, and the potential for pain, this is definitely a time when you want to have really clear conversations about what you are OK and not OK about doing.

168

Pleasure, not pain

My friend said, 'Oh my god, I had (penis-in-vagina) sex and it was so painful.' And then she looked me in the eye and said, 'It'll make you cry, Madeleine.' And that has always stuck in my mind. And so I just didn't. I was 20 when I first had sex. It wasn't painful in the least. *Madeleine, 28*

You might be worried about penis-in-vagina (PIV) sex if you haven't done it before, or if you have a new partner. You might think that the penis is going to be too big, that the vagina is too small or that the hymen is going to rip or bleed. These are *extremely* unlikely!

However, research shows that people with penises AND people with vaginas do sometimes find PIV sex painful. The thing is, it's not supposed to be!

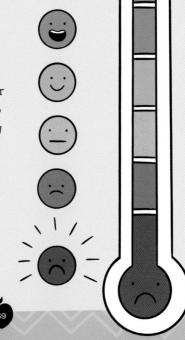

If it hurts, then something isn't working, and you should stop and try something else instead:

★ Try not to stress about it – it can happen even to people who are very experienced.

★ Talk about it – when and where it hurt.

★ Go slower, and maybe shift positions to find something comfortable.

★ You can say, 'Hey, stop,' or 'That doesn't feel good,' or 'Can we try a different position?'

★ Help each other out by asking, 'Shall we try this angle/ position?' or 'I'd like to move up/down/to this side to see how that feels – is that OK?'

★ Lubrication is a crucial prerequisite for comfortable, pleasurable intercourse. The vagina-owner must be really turned on to get natural lubrication going. The penis-owner needs to be aroused and fully erect. You may need to use extra lube with a condom.

★ Even with plenty of lubrication, the sensation of the penis touching the opening of the vagina can cause the muscles around the vagina to tighten reflexively. If the penis isn't erect enough, or if it's pushed in hard without the vagina being lubricated, it can also cause pain in the penis. For young people, painful penis-in-vagina sex is usually because of these 'mechanical' reasons. (See Is something wrong? on page 260.)

Dry sex

❝ I've been going out with my boyfriend for three and a half months now. We're both in Year Eight and he recently turned 13, while I'm almost 14. We're going to see a movie soon and he said he wants to have dry sex? ❞

This usually means people having intercourse with clothes or underwear on. It can also mean humping, or 'going through the motions' (e.g. rubbing genitals together and moving or thrusting in sync) without actually getting to penetration. For example, rubbing genitals together and moving or thrusting without putting the penis inside. It can be super sexy and pleasurable for many couples and part of mixing up different ways to have sex. Some might choose dry sex to avoid the risk of pregnancy. Some might choose it to make sex last hours. It's legal for consenting teens as it doesn't involve penetration.

Mutual masturbation

> My boyfriend and I haven't really done mutual masturbation! It's not on the list of things to do. I haven't heard much about it. Oh, is it where you touch EACH OTHER?! LOL. Yes. I have done that. I find it more enjoyable than penetration! *Phoebe, 17*

Mutual masturbation can be one of the most delightful and fun ways to have sex with other people! And it's just what it sounds like – touching each other's genitals for sexual pleasure, either at the same time, or one after the other, or swapping back and forth. Mutual masturbation might involve fingering or a hand job (see pages 154 and 158) or both, depending on what genital parts you and your partner have. Exploring each other's bodies with your hands can be extremely pleasurable.

It's good to check in with each other about what feels good and what you want more or less of. Just as you get to know your own body when you masturbate solo, doing this with a partner helps you get to know each other's bodies and discover what they like and don't like. And don't forget – clean hands!

Nudes, texting and online sex

66 What is phone sex? All the girls at school keep talking about it and I'm too embarrassed to say I don't know, help! 99

66 My crush has been talking to me for the last few months and he also has a crush on me. He asked for nudes and at first I didn't want to send them but then I did. He sent some back and IDK what to do because I'm scared about facing him at school and I've even been skipping class. 99

Getting sexy with another person can also happen when you're physically separated from them. Back in the days before phones, people wrote letters – *love letters!* Fast forward about 150 years and communication can happen in milliseconds, 24/7.

Sexy texting (sometimes called 'sexting') involves sending a sexy message, picture or video of yourself to another person with your smartphone or computer. Sexting might go back and forth between you and another person like a conversation, or it might just happen occasionally or once. A 'nude' is a sext that involves a naked photo of you or part of your body – such as your genitals.

Like any other type of sex with another person, you'll have things you like and don't like when it comes to doing stuff online. If you're having online sex, it's just as important as for in-person sex to be in control, to feel respected and to give and receive consent. It's not OK for someone to send you nudes out of the blue, or if you don't want to receive them! And you don't have to send any if you don't want to.

IF WE WERE TALKING TO OUR OWN KIDS, WE'D TELL THEM TO ALWAYS CROP THEIR HEADS OUT OF ANY PHOTOS, JUST IN CASE – BECAUSE ONCE A PIC IS OUT THERE, YOU HAVE NO CONTROL OVER WHO WILL SEE IT.

Sexting and the law

Special laws apply when it comes to sharing nude pics. Sharing private material without consent is a crime and you can report it to the police. The laws are there to protect young people and children from being abused by adults, but it can get messy if you or your partner are under 18. That's because nudes of people under 18 are considered 'child pornography' by the law in the UK & Ireland.

IF YOU SEND A NUDE WITH SOMEONE YOU'RE BEING INTIMATE WITH, THEY AREN'T ALLOWED TO SHARE IT WITH ANYONE ELSE WITHOUT YOUR CONSENT, AND VICE VERSA – IT CAN BE A CRIME.

Is this different from phone sex?

Yes – phone sex is when people talk on the phone in a sexual way, getting each other turned on. You might speak about what you would do to each other's bodies if you were physically together, or describe a sexy situation to each other. Each person's body gets aroused and they might start touching themselves – like mutual masturbation while apart (see Mutual masturbation on page 172). Since smartphones are actually mini-computers and camera-phones, phone sex these days crosses over into 'online sex' (aka cybersex).

Aftercare

Aftercare is about checking in with yourself and your partner straight after you've had sex or tried something sexual. It doesn't matter if they're a long-term partner or someone you had a casual hook-up with. This can be something physical, like a cuddle or snuggle, before falling asleep. It can be as straightforward as saying, 'Are you OK?' or 'Was that OK?' Maybe it's having a laugh and a pillow fight, taking a shower together, the stroke of a hand, or going outside and sitting in the sunshine (or moonshine). It might be asking 'How are you feeling?' and having a chat – about anything – or just being in each other's presence. Aftercare following a casual hook-up might be sending a message later and acknowledging the other person's humanity.

I really like aftercare. I'm always in a hurry to get dressed and get back into my comfortable clothes but my bf just loves to lie around naked. And I'm like, 'I can see your butt!' And he'll jiggle it and wiggle it. *Phoebe, 17*

Sometimes sex can bring up big emotions – some people burst into huge tears after an orgasm! It's not that anything bad has happened, it's that we feel like we left the earth for a time, and now we need to be gently held as we return back down.

Aftercare is important. It's not bad if you cry after sex, it's emotional. *Jessie. 23*

Why does aftercare matter? Simple answer – because we're humans, not robots. For most people, even the most fleeting of sexual encounters still makes us feel a connection. It's good to know the other person felt something too, or that they acknowledge you exist.

If you're in a long-term relationship with a person, aftercare means letting each other know that whether it's the first or hundredth moment of intimacy, you both felt a sense of togetherness.

WOBBLY STARTS

66 My boyfriend and I are at a steady stage of our relationship and we have decided we want to have sex. I am a little nervous about this because I'm not sure I'll know what to do. I have very little knowledge on sexual matters and am really desperate for some answers. 99

66 My girlfriend and I have been together for ages and are ready to make things more physical, but every time we go to do 'it' (penis-in-vagina sex), I get really nervous and kind of lose my mojo. I feel like she has all these expectations and I won't live up to them. What should I do? 99

Getting off to a wobbly start is common when you're learning something new. Picture a baby taking its first couple of steps, and then – plonk! Back on their bum! Or manoeuvring a new wheelchair around the school corridors – maybe a side-swipe is to be expected. Our bodies are good at learning new skills and adapting to different situations, but they take practice.

Becoming sexually intimate with another person for the first time is also about learning something new. Yes, physically – but emotionally, too! You learn new things about yourself and about the other person. It's hard to predict how you'll feel both during and after an intimate act. You might find yourself thinking differently about your body or identity, for instance. You might have surprised yourself. Or you might think sex is a bit of an anticlimax – and that's OK, too.

Expectations and disappointment

So much of what we see or hear about sex creates a huge set of expectations. This means a lot of early sexual experiences can end up feeling disappointing. That sense of disappointment can quickly turn into worry, mortification, guilt or something equally unhelpful, like, 'Eek! There's something wrong with me!' Or 'Eek! there's something wrong with my partner!' You don't really know how to process the experience because you haven't had a lot of sex at this point.

Every expert we interviewed for this book talked about how people can become anxious about sex because of what they believe is **expected of them** or of their partners.

Lots of teens have also told us that although their first experiences of sex were OK, or even pretty good, it didn't match what they'd **expected**.

So it's time to change expectations!

Sex shouldn't be like going into a restaurant and ordering the fixed menu. Some people don't want dessert, or all three courses. Sex should be a picnic, where you can choose what you want. Maybe you only want to try some of the dips, maybe you'll save the pavlova for next time. There shouldn't be this expectation that you have to reach some goal or it's a failure. It should be about 'What am I feeling in this moment and what am I wanting?' *Jacqueline Hellyer, sex therapist*

Sex is not necessarily going to be good the first time – it's going to be awkward. It's going to be, you know ... weird. Especially if you're having sex with someone who's the opposite gender and you've never seen whatever it is that they've got! Because, at the end of the day, you do what you're most comfortable with, you explore with that other person, and if that other person's not making you feel confident about your body or what it is that you're experiencing, then that's not sex anymore. *Lisa, 23*

Oops, fail!

OK, so you and your partner were psyched up for some first-time intimacy. And, oops, it didn't quite work out. Maybe one or both of you just didn't get aroused, or maybe it was all over really quickly, or you couldn't figure out *what* to do when – and it ended up way more awkward than you hoped. Maybe you were nervous.

SITUATIONS LIKE THIS HAPPEN EVEN WHEN YOU FEEL FULLY PREPARED. IT CAN HAPPEN TO ANYONE – IT'S NORMAL WHEN YOU'RE STARTING OUT (AND ALSO WHEN YOU'RE FULLY EXPERIENCED)!

While nerves or self-consciousness can contribute, sometimes it's just a wobbly start and doesn't need a reason.

Try not to stress. Have a laugh about it with your partner. Think about the bigger picture – you actually got intimate with someone, and it was exciting! Fun! Maybe it was loving and caring. Maybe it felt like a new kind of connection with another human being. Or maybe you just realised they weren't the right partner for you after all, and that's fine, too. Focus on what felt good – physically and emotionally – and savour those feelings.

He barely made it in before he came. I think he was really embarrassed and I was like, 'It's okaaaay!' I thought it was funny. There was lots of kindness between us; it was a good experience. It felt like it was the right thing for us. It took a while for it to get good. For the first few months it was still a bit awkward, because we didn't know what we were doing. Practice made it better. *Gemma*

Anticlimactic sex

Sex can literally be an anticlimax, meaning no climax (ejaculation or orgasm)! Totally common. Or it might be that the experience itself was an anticlimax – meaning 'a disappointing end after an exciting series of events'.

Don't stress if this happened. There are lots of reasons why sex can be anticlimactic. It might be that each of you was aroused and that things you and your partner did were coordinated and felt good – but then one or both of you didn't reach a physical climax. Maybe something happened midway that put you off, and no matter what, there was no way for you to get your head back in the game!

For people with a penis, perhaps your erection went down quicker than you wanted, or maybe you ejaculated earlier than you'd hoped. For people with a vagina and clitoris, orgasm might not have happened despite trying. Sometimes it just doesn't!

Perhaps each partner did 'climax' but it still felt unsatisfying. After all, when we see a sexual climax portrayed in the movies or online, it looks and sounds so incredible! And maybe what you experienced was kinda 'meh'.

A powerful stereotype about sex is that it is all about the climax – a physical, mind-blowing orgasm. And if one or both partners don't achieve that, it's seen as some sort of huge failure or disappointment. But that's simply not true.

There is no formula you have to follow, no single finish-line you have to reach. The same goes for your partner. Because sex is new, the stakes feel high. As you get older, you realise you get multiple chances to get it 'right'. And hitting some bum notes (lol) is actually part of the process.

I feel like an orgasm gives the other person validation that they've done the right thing and if there's no orgasm they might think they've done the wrong thing or they're not good enough. People connect orgasms to validation. *Phoebe. 17*

GLADYS'S STORY – A WOBBLY START

My first time I was 18. I thought I was behind because when I was in high school I had friends who were already having sex in Year Eight. It blew my mind as I didn't get how they could be mature enough! My Year 12 boyfriend – we did things … but we didn't do THAT.

My first time wasn't great! I was hungover for the very first time and feeling rebellious. He came over to my house without my family there. I was so horny. I didn't know why. And I was like, 'This is gonna be the day that we have sex.'

I knew where I could get condoms in the house, but I made us walk to the shops to get condoms because I was too nervous and was trying to put it off. When we got back to the house, I suggested we watch a movie, again trying to put it off! I made him watch *Mean Girls* – the entire movie. And he sat so still. I think he was thinking, 'What the f*** is happening?' When the film ended I thought, 'Oh no, now what!' We ended up having penetrative sex and it was just fine. It didn't blow my mind. It was awkward and not what I thought it was going to be. By the time we got to it the whole feeling was lost, we weren't in the mood anymore! My advice looking back would just be like, get it done when you have that horny feeling! I psyched myself out. (That happens now! As an adult!)

My folks came home and he forgot to leave because we fell asleep! So I hid him in my cupboard. WE WERE 18. Technically adults! But I made him hide for two hours until I snuck him downstairs and then he rang the doorbell and acted like he'd just arrived.

We dated for another year and the sex didn't really improve. We had to sneak around and not get caught. I think I wasn't really attracted to him. It was like puppy love.

Lack of orgasm

❝ I've been having sex with my boyfriend for about three months now (he is my first). We do it quite frequently but I still haven't had an orgasm. What is wrong with me? **❞**

Lack of orgasm was a common reason that teen girls (who had had penis-in-vagina sex) wrote into Dolly Doctor. This happened with penis-in-vagina sex, when the vagina-owner didn't orgasm or wasn't sure how to. Heartbreakingly, most, if not all, of these teens thought there was something wrong with them.

Research tells us that when heterosexual couples have sex, there is a huge 'orgasm gap', where almost 100 per cent of men have an orgasm, but less than two-thirds of women do. This gap isn't there when the sex is between two women. And women having solo sex tend to have no problem reaching orgasm! So **it isn't that women can't orgasm.** It's that during penis-vagina sex, female pleasure is not prioritised enough.

Your fingers and mouth are your best friend when you're trying to pleasure a girl. Penetration isn't everything! Relax – if you're stressed out and feeling anxious, it's not fun for anyone. *Josh, 19*

To make a start at CLOSING the orgasm gap, it's important to understand that **everyone has an equal right to pleasure**. Girls are not meant to passively 'cop' whatever is done to them by their male partners. Figuring out what brings *you* pleasure and learning what brings *your partner* pleasure is part of the joy of sex. It may mean reassessing the spread on the picnic table with fresh eyes! Feeling safe is an underrated element in enjoying sex and getting to orgasm. Feeling like you don't have to look pretty and be 'hot' or 'perfect', and feeling like you have the freedom to be loud and messy, will help close that orgasm gap.

Like driving: you get better at it

Have you noticed there are more restrictions on young drivers when they first get their licence? You can't go too fast, or drive after drinking alcohol, for instance. Driving a car can feel powerful and awesome, but it also makes you vulnerable in new ways. The aim is to get from A to B, while also making sure your passengers and others on the road are safe. It's about your driving skill, but also about your awareness of others around you.

It was as successful as a first time could be. It wasn't too long! There were good laughs throughout. *Seb, 19*

Sex is more complicated than driving a car, but, like driving, it's something that gets better with experience and practice. Your nerves die down, your sense of urgency and stress start to settle, and you can take time to enjoy the scenery, not rush, and be thoughtful and considerate to others! Toot toot!

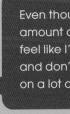

Even though I've had a decent amount of experience, I still feel like I'm making it up a bit and don't know what's going on a lot of the time. *Tiger, 19*

It's important to remember that there is no **one way** to have sex, or to enjoy it. Even more important than figuring out what your body can do is getting to know your feelings and thoughts, and how they can change in different situations. Learning to communicate with a partner and getting to know them also helps build confidence, trust and respect – for them and for yourself.

RELATIONSHIPS

A relationship is a connection between you and another person – that person could be a good friend, team mate, sibling, parent or trusted adult. Some teens discover **romantic** relationships, which are new and different. As you probably guessed, they involve a romantic element – big feelings of love and attraction. They might be expressed through holding hands, kissing or other physical touch. Parents/carers, other family members, peers and others will influence the kinds of relationships we prioritise.

> My Asian mum would not say the word 'sex' in my household. If there was a sex scene even in a family movie on TV I had to cover my face with a pillow! My brother too. They would say, 'No! No!' and grab the pillow. *Gladys*

Some teens have romantic relationships that don't involve sex. Some teens want to have sex with others but aren't interested in being in a relationship with them. Not everyone is going to be interested in romantic or sexual relationships. Others will LIVE for this stuff! So don't worry if your friends are in romantic relationships and you're not. Romantic relationships are not more valid than friendship relationships.

Why are romantic relationships so confusing?

Romantic relationships can be long or short and can happen between people of any gender. As teens get older, their romantic relationships may also involve sex. Regardless of whether the couple is having sex, a romantic relationship can be confusing because of all the big feelings involved – especially when your hormones have such a huge influence on your emotions! Navigating a romantic relationship involves thinking about how the other person feels, how you feel, and how they all tie in together, which can be tricky at any age. Sex can amplify emotions, making things trickier again.

Here are some of the many questions sent to Dolly Doctor about romantic relationships.

QUESTIONS FOR DR MELISSA

66 So, I'm in this friendship group with three girls including myself. I recently found out Taylah has a crush on Jess, but Jess doesn't know. I'm scared that if Jess finds out, they might start dating and I'll just be third-wheeling like my whole life. And what if our friendship group breaks up?? Help!! 99

66 I'm 13 and I had a crush for almost two years and suddenly he asked me out. We dated for a little bit, then he said he doesn't want to date me until school starts (it's summer holidays), and then a few weeks later he said he missed me and loved me and asked me out again, and then he said he wants to be single for the holidays, but he said he still loves me. I don't know how to feel about this and is this good or bad? 99

66 I have a boyfriend who I have been dating for more than a year and a half, and also another guy who I have always been close with. He told me that he has very strong feelings for me and I think I have them back. However, I still am really close with my boyfriend. What should I do?? **99**

66 I have this friend who I care about so much, but the things that she and her boyfriend do are things that I definitely DON'T agree with! They are only 15 (so am I) and to make matters worse her parents have no idea they are even dating, plus, I don't trust her boyfriend one bit! I'm concerned for her but I don't know how to tell her! **99**

Here's a tip: the people you're flirting with, kissing or crushing on are just as confused as you. Them saying one thing, then doing the opposite – changing their minds or just being UNPREDICTABLE – is part of *their* puberty journey! It's not your fault and you're probably not imagining it!

The big thing we keep talking about in this book is the importance of communicating. Asking things like: 'Do you like me?', 'Does it feel good when I do this?', 'How would you like it if I kissed you?' or 'Do you want to go steady?' This takes courage! It can be really scary – and, like driving, and making out, and getting along with your teachers, it can take practice. You won't be perfect at it straight away. If you have questions and you don't understand what's going on, you can say it.

Hey, I don't get it. Are we flirting?

Are you doing this because you like me?

Can I tell you what I'm looking for in a relationship?

Would you be offended if I told you I was in love with you?

Do you know how cute it is to me when you do that?

Their answer might not necessarily be the one you want to hear. But by asking, you're taking huge steps towards figuring things out AND you're practising those communication skills!

Research tells us that teens experience 'highs' and 'lows' more intensely compared to older people. But just because you're young, that doesn't mean your big feelings aren't real! They absolutely ARE. There is a lot going on inside your body that sends all kinds of messages to your heart and your brain that aren't logical and that you probably can't explain – but the feelings are still real.

If the people you're having big feelings for are your age, they're probably going through the same big ups and downs that you are – so you can't predict what they're going to do!

GIVE YOURSELF TIME TO RIDE IT OUT AND REMEMBER THAT, NO MATTER HOW BAD YOU'RE FEELING, THE FEELING WILL PASS.

Dating

QUESTIONS FOR DR MELISSA

❝ I'm 14, so there's this guy and he really likes me and he is always telling me how much he loves me and he's always calling me beautiful. He really wants to date me but I'm still not sure if I like him enough to date him. But the thing is that I have times where I really like him and then there's times when he just gets annoying! I'm just not sure if I'm ready!!! What should I do? **❞**

For some teens, 'dating' means the same thing as being in a steady relationship. For others, it might mean seeing someone occasionally, like hanging out, but as more than friends. It might be like a rehearsal for a more full-on relationship. There can be different levels of attraction, even between the same two people, and this uncertainty can be confusing – but it can also be exciting!

Dating can also mean going out on dates with people you don't know. Dating apps are designed for young and older adults to find other people to meet and go on a date with. This kind of dating doesn't have to involve sex either.

A lot of dating, especially in the teen years, doesn't involve sex. Dating can mean that you and someone else agree that you're romantically interested in each other – 'going steady' or 'hooked up' – and spend time together. It could involve hanging out together at school. It could be seeing each other outside of school, or going on dates, or holding hands. It could also happen online. Most teens have their first experiences of physical intimacy with someone they're dating in this way. Dating can be fun and exciting, but it can also kick off some real worries!

Hooking up

> After high school finished, I had sex for the first time with a close friend of mine, and it felt really safe and comfortable because we had that trust with each other. *Tiger, 19*

Like lots of things about sex, hooking up can also mean different things to different people. For many teens, 'hooking up' involves intimate stuff – this could be kissing, cuddling or making out. It might be sexual touching, oral sex, getting naked or having intercourse. **Hooking up happens between people who are not in a relationship with each other.** They might be friends or relative strangers. Sometimes people hook up unexpectedly in the moment. Other times it might be sort of planned, or hoped for.

Hooking up probably starts in late high school and beyond. Hook-up culture is so predominant now, I think that meaningful connection has got lost. There's a culture where you feel used and aren't valued. This affects women disproportionately. Hook-up means different things – it could just be touching another person's body, it could be nudity, it could be intercourse. Definitions keep changing. *Dominique. 17*

There's a lot of pressure for younger people (teens to early 20s) to feel like, in order to have lived a life, they need to be involved in hook-up culture. But I think it is, like all things related to sex, a preference thing. And some people like it and some don't. Personally, I'm more comfortable if I know the person. I feel weird getting naked and vulnerable in front of someone I don't know! *Madeleine. 28*

199

What are the rules of (intimate) relationships?

This is one of the most frequently asked questions about relationships! Figuring them out is also like being on your L-plates. It can be fun and exhilarating some of the time, and stressful or mind-numbingly complicated at other times.

> My first boyfriend and I were such good friends and just LIKED each other so much as people ... We found each other really funny and were able to be open with each other about sex. We also had those big swoony, crushy feelings. *Angie, 43*

There's no 'formula' for figuring out when and how intimate relationships work, although respect and honesty are a great starting point! Each person needs to set their own boundaries, and those boundaries need to be respected. These boundaries can act like rules for a relationship, and they can change over time. If it's all still pretty new, there are some things you could ask yourself.

WHY DO I WANT TO BE IN A RELATIONSHIP?

- ✦ Do I feel pressured by my peers or another person?

- ✦ Do I want to impress others or feel like I 'belong'?

- ✦ Am I interested in and attracted to this other person and want to get to know them better?

- ✦ Am I willing and able to give this other person my time and attention?

AM I COMFORTABLE WITH WHO I AM?

- ✦ Do I believe I can be my genuine self with this other person?

- ✦ Am I happy on my own, but want to share my interests and time with this other person?

Building a healthy relationship

Getting into a new intimate or romantic relationship can be like walking on clouds, and full of suffocatingly happy, horny, magical feelings. One way to 'care' for a relationship even from the early, heady days is to try to pace things – take the time to get to know the other person better and more deeply, and don't focus just on what you find superficially attractive. Pay attention to your own feelings, too, as you gradually open up more about yourself. Enjoy those moments of a growing friendship as well as something romantic and intimate.

Teen relationships can be really rewarding. You have someone to text, check in on, someone to go to a formal with – a confidante. Some of these relationships become blueprints for how we act for the rest of our lives. But don't forget you're still figuring things out. In a lot of cases, you're following the examples set by parents/carers. Sometimes that's great, and sometimes they aren't necessarily what we'd choose if we really thought about it!

Going slowly and building trust over time is definitely important. Communicating what they're comfortable with. Also asking them how they're doing can help build that trust and reassure them that you care. *Josh, 17*

Figuring out how to communicate with each other is one of the healthiest things we can all do in relationships, whether it's with your annoying younger sibling, your parents or your new romantic partner! Communication challenges might occur when people don't know each other well and feel awkward or shy, when they speak different languages or come from different cultures, when they have different communication abilities or when one or more people feel vulnerable for whatever reason.

TRUST

COMMUNICATION

RESPECT

COMMUNICATING WITH YOUR PARTNER IS IMPORTANT FOR SHOWING CARE AND RESPECT, FOR ASKING FOR AND GIVING CONSENT TO DO INTIMATE THINGS TOGETHER, AND FOR FIGURING OUT THE 'RULES' YOU EACH WANT AS YOUR RELATIONSHIP GROWS.

CARE

Cheating

66 I don't know what to do about my ex. He's constantly in my dreams and on my mind even though I know he lied and that he even cheated on me. 99

66 The guy I like, who wants to (have sex), seems to use me but every time I confront him he says he's not! So I am SO confused! And we are not even going out – he's going out with another girl! So he's basically cheating! 99

66 I have a bf who I really love and I don't know what I'll do without him. He recently cheated on me with another girl, and I forgave him. But now I don't think I can trust him. He told me if I broke up with him he'll never love another girl the way he loved me and that he'll keep coming back to me. But I keep getting hurt by him ... WHAT DO I DO!!! Please help me. 99

What counts as cheating depends on the **expectations** in the relationship. For some, cheating might include flirting with another person. For others, cheating means touching someone in a sexual way, kissing or sexual intercourse. In early high school, 'cheating' often means kissing or making out with someone else outside of the relationship.

Cheating usually means **breaking a relationship rule**. If you had an understanding that while you were together you weren't going to kiss anyone else, and someone breaks that rule, that's cheating.

It affects people in different ways – from feeling angry to heartbroken to disrespected, to not overly bothered! A lot of relationships end because of cheating, but not always … It's one of the tricky things to figure out!

Breaking up

66 I have fallen in love with a German exchange (student) who has fallen in love with me too. So we decided to be in a relationship. But I am worried because I have another seven months with him, and I don't know if he wants to break up after he goes. And I would like to try long-distance because it may or may not work. And it's worrying me. 99

66 I'm in a situation. I have a boyfriend and lately we have been drifting apart. We don't talk as much or hang out anymore. I also have a close friend who I think I might be developing a crush on. My boyfriend's sister and I are really close and I worry that if I break it off with him, I will lose her as my friend. I'm not sure how I'm feeling about my boyfriend and I don't know what I should do and how I should do it. Please help! 99

Most relationships during the teen years are passionate, but they're not built to last. So breaking up is pretty common!

A 'good' break-up might still hurt, but afterwards each person appreciates what was good about the relationship, and feels OK that it's over.

Other break-ups suck! It's much harder when one person is still very in love and the other isn't. It's also harder if there's been bad communication, like they blame you for the break-up, talk smack about you when it's over, or get someone else to tell you. Worst of all, when they tell you nothing at all and ghost you.

Being blamed or disrespected in the break-up can also make it more painful and make you wonder or worry about what went wrong.

MORE ON p. 210

Dealing with a broken heart

66 I need help! My boyfriend broke up with me a few days ago and it's really hard for me to get over him! How do I move on from someone who I've been dating for a year? **99**

66 My friend is going through a rough time after a break-up. He loves her and can't get over her. What would be the best advice for him getting over her?? **99**

66 (After) an unexpected break-up, I was so distraught and I felt so empty and heartbroken. I felt like I was dying inside. **99**

Some of the world's best songs have been written by someone with a broken heart. Having a broken heart can really hurt – and healing can't be rushed.

Think about what you liked about yourself when you were with that person. Can you nurture that version of you? Heartbreak is brutal, but it helps you understand the stakes of a romantic relationship. The pain is real! And trust us, it is something you can get over – eventually you'll come away from it feeling happier and stronger.

My lover in high school couldn't come out as gay and that really affected her and she ended it between us. And then she got together with my best buddy, who was a guy! That broke my heart. *Alex-Rose, 50*

I tried to dismiss it like, 'I'm young and I knew this was coming so I shouldn't be sad.' And I tried to make it like my sadness was about something else. But it was about the END OF MY RELATIONSHIP. *Phoebe, 17*

I had been sad before and had big break-ups, but never that heart-wrenching and desperate pain of break-up. So it was like when you've had a cold and you think it's the flu, but then you get the real flu and you realise you'd had no idea what flu was. I was physically sick during my last break-up. I literally felt pain in my heart. *Anonymous*

Ghosting

I got ghosted. We'd had this hot fling. I thought it was real. He said he had to go away for a week and I was like, 'Oh, that's sad, see ya when you get back,' and then he never answered my messages EVER AGAIN! It was rough. I spent so much energy wondering what the hell had happened, hoping he hadn't DIED, wondering if he'd maybe lost my details …?! The confusion was excruciating. Years later I ran into him and asked, and yeah, he'd had another girl and chosen the better option. *Yumi*

Being ghosted sucks.

Ghosting is when you completely blank the other person you connected with and act like they don't exist, instead of telling them that you're not ready for anything more or you want it to end. Ghosting is often sudden or a bit of a surprise – and it leaves the other person trying to figure out why they didn't even deserve a 'goodbye' text. It's pretty cowardly.

The ghoster could be scared of having difficult conversations, or being in a situation with big emotions. Sometimes they're just massive jerks. Sometimes they're playing a numbers game with multiple partners until one pays off. If you're ready for any kind of intimacy with another person, even if it's casual and fun, then you should also be able to respectfully say goodbye.

If you've been ghosted, you have the right to want an explanation – just know that you might not get one.

RELATIONSHIPS ARE NOT FOR EVERYONE!

If you've been thinking, 'What the heck?! I have zero interest in relationships or love or romance' – there's nothing wrong! They're just not for you – and that's OK.

Respectful relationships

Whatever a relationship looks like for you, a respectful one is the only one worth having. Seriously. Just started going steady with someone in your class? Yay! Just wanna have fun exploring sexy stuff with others? Sure. Fallen out of love with the person you've been dating for a year? OK.

Whatever kind of sex you are having or WISH to have, it doesn't exist without emotion. People have sex because they want to feel a connection. For the connection to be fulfilling, you need to connect with someone who respects you and who you respect.

A good way to figure it out sometimes is to ask yourself, 'How would I want someone to treat my best friend in this situation?' And if you wouldn't let them be treated badly, then don't let yourself either!

Start with valuing yourself and the other person. See yourselves as equals. Know what you want and be willing to listen to what they want. Communicating what's good and what isn't. Knowing your boundaries and accepting theirs.

Cancelling an agreed meet-up at short notice without a good reason is a pretty clear sign that they don't respect me. *Yumi*

How they treat you in front of their friends is so important! If they're dismissive of you because their mates are around? Walk away. *Anouk, 20*

An ideal world, when it comes to sex, is one where people know how to BE HUMAN! They respect themselves and each other, or, more to the point, men respect women and women respect themselves. They learn honesty – they learn to be more open, communicate more so there is less guesswork, they talk about what they like and don't like. You don't have to be in a relationship with someone to have sex with them, and you might not have any expectation of a 'next time'. But NO ghosting. Just be a decent person. *Natalie, 28*

MADELEINE'S STORY

I don't think sex is that different when you're disabled. You just need to find what works for you. There's a misconception that sex with disabled people is really complicated and lacks intimacy, or that disabled people have no sexual feelings at all. But that's not true. There are lots of disabled people enjoying lots of different kinds of sex.

The biggest misconception when it comes to disabled sex is the idea that disabled people should only go out with other disabled people. Even my adult friends are struggling with that – where our friends and families just assume that the only people who would want to date people with disability are other people with disability. It's OK if you want to date someone with a disability, but it should be open that we can date everybody and that everybody should be comfortable with dating us!

My disabled friends would prefer to go out with someone who has a sense of the disabled community – whether they're disabled or not, they need to have an understanding of disability. It's vital that the people we date need to understand us and our needs, listen to us and respect us.

My current (non-disabled) partner has a brother with autism, so he understands the disabled experience and doesn't see disability as a barrier to love. Disability shouldn't be such a divider that you can't date us, and it doesn't make us subhuman! Everyone wants to be loved and feel that connection.

I think for some people who don't understand, there is a divide of disabled and non-disabled bodies and disabled sexiness and non-disabled sexiness. They think there is a

difference. But for people in the loop, in the know, they realise there isn't any difference. Every human on this planet is different! Whether you have a disability or not.

Madeleine Stewart, 28, disabled comedian

WHAT'S YOUR ADVICE TO A YOUNG DISABLED PERSON?

Don't be too hard on yourself and your body. A lot of teenagers have complicated feelings about the way their body looks. Especially teenagers with disability, but that's normal. It's part of being a teenager – you're figuring things out. You might not even want to identify as disabled, and that's all right too! I was so hard on myself as a teenager! I thought, If I looked nicer, if I had better clothes, maybe people would like me. But remember – everyone is just as nervous, scared and self-conscious as you are.

You will be loved! You are worthy of love! And even if you feel like you live in a world that doesn't love you, don't settle for second best.

LOOKING AFTER MYSELF AND MY PARTNER

Sex is something that should make you feel happy. That means really *enjoying* moments of intimacy with another person. It also means feeling respected and understanding you have the right to pleasure. So much of this depends on how you and your partner feel emotionally and your communication before, during and after sex. When health professionals talk about being 'sexually healthy', they mean having a sense of wellbeing that is **physical**, **emotional**, **mental** and **social**. Sexual health is about the whole you!

Avoiding any unwanted physical consequences of sex, such as pregnancy and sexually transmitted infections (STIs), is also part of sexual health. It's about each person taking responsibility for looking after themselves AND their partner, each time they have sex.

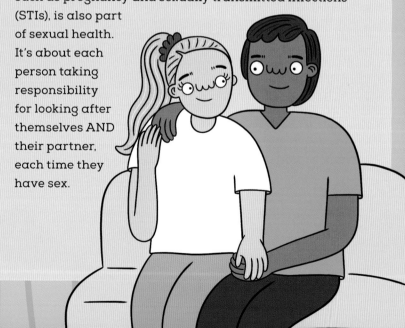

I thought school sex ed was pretty shit. I was at an all-girls school so you'd think it'd be more of a safe space to ask questions and stuff, but it was so basic you didn't learn anything you didn't already know. *Gemma*

Sex ed doesn't generally deal effectively with trans teens well. It can trigger gender dysphoria, because young people mostly learn about contraception and STIs for cisgender people. Trans teens are at a higher risk to have an unplanned pregnancy, STIs or HIV compared to cisgender teens and sex ed is often not relevant for young trans people. *Cristyn Davies, researcher and advocate*

Both of the schools I have been to have strong advocacy of abstinence: 'Don't have sex, you'll get sick, you'll get pregnant, you'll die!' Some people took it into consideration but were like, WE CAN'T BE DYING FROM THIS, THAT CAN'T BE TRUE. *Charlotte, 17*

The **only** type of sex where pregnancy is likely to happen is when a penis goes into a vagina, squirts sperm-containing semen inside, and a sperm then finds an egg within the uterus or the Fallopian tubes. It **doesn't** happen from kissing, oral sex, mutual masturbation, sexual touching, anal sex, sperm swimming in a swimming pool towards you, or fingering or using a sex toy inside a vagina (unless there's lots of fresh sperm on the finger or toy – even so, the chances are not high).

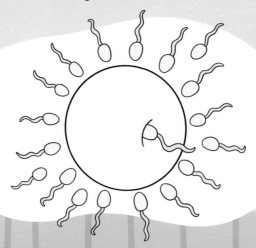

From the time that humans figured this out, they started inventing all sorts of ways to stop pregnancy from happening. Why? Because sex is pleasurable, fun, intimate, joyful, loving ... and it's great to be able to enjoy sex without worrying whether a pregnancy will occur. For thousands of years, there weren't a lot of options when it came to contraception. Luckily, for the past few generations, medical technology has greatly increased the birth control options available – and, importantly, dramatically improved their effectiveness.

Different types of contraception work on different parts of the 'how pregnancy-from-sex happens' chain. Here are some examples:

MORE ON p. 236

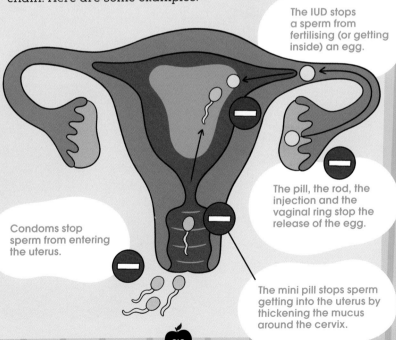

The IUD stops a sperm from fertilising (or getting inside) an egg.

The pill, the rod, the injection and the vaginal ring stop the release of the egg.

Condoms stop sperm from entering the uterus.

The mini pill stops sperm getting into the uterus by thickening the mucus around the cervix.

Contraception

❝ I want to know if you have sex in a pool with a condom (on) is it still possible to get pregnant because the sperm from the condom could somehow swim in the water and in (to) the vagina? **❞**

❝ Is there any chance of getting pregnant during oral sex? **❞**

Contraception, sometimes called 'birth control', is what people do to avoid pregnancy when they have sex.

Growing up in Dominican Republic I quickly learned that getting pregnant was an impediment to going out and living your life for girls. Always four or five girls got pregnant before ending high school, in *every* year level. That's one of the reasons I never had sex before leaving high school – because I was very afraid of getting pregnant! *Rocio Marte, 40*

Barrier contraception

Condoms are called 'barrier' contraceptives, because they put up a physical barrier between sperm and egg. Modern-day condoms are an incredible technological invention – they can actually stop microscopic, invisible sperm and virus particles and bacteria getting through them. This is the only contraception that also prevents STI transmission. If the condom breaks or slips, oops – bye-bye, barrier!

Condoms designed to fit on a penis are called 'external condoms' (or 'male condoms'), while those designed to fit inside a vagina are called 'internal condoms' (or 'female condoms'). It's much more common for young people to use male condoms – they are easier to find and they're cheaper than female condoms.

The first time I bought condoms I was 14. There used to be a servo down the road from my house. I was like, 'I don't want to JUST buy condoms' so I also bought a chocolate milk! My friends were like, 'Are you even allowed to buy condoms when you're 14?' The cashier didn't say anything. I had a bit of nerves buying them because I'd never done it before, but it went very normally. *Declan, 19*

Condoms are sexy!

'Condoms kill the vibe' is a common myth that we'd like to see gently exfoliated off the face of the Earth. We get that learning to put a condom on a banana in sex ed can seem a bit weird. But it's actually a useful way to get kids familiar with touching and handling condoms so they seem LESS weird when the time comes to use one during sex.

Humans have used condoms since ancient times so that they could enjoy sex. That's right! The whole point of condoms is to allow people to have enjoyable sex without having to stress about pregnancy and STIs. A condom doesn't kill the vibe – but worrying about the consequences of sex will! So use a condom, and enjoy yourself!

Condoms are surprisingly easy to use! I assumed that they were illegal to buy when I was little, LOL. So the biggest hurdle was buying them! I had to do the whole classic Buying Other Things with the condoms so I didn't feel any shame, and the world didn't end so I was OK.
Phoebe, 17

Male condoms, aka 'condoms'

Male condoms are popular with
Australian teens. Research shows
that three-quarters of teens used
male condoms the first time they had penis-in-vagina sex.

Male condoms are sold in supermarkets, pharmacies,
petrol stations and vending machines. Some sexual
health and youth centres give away free condoms. They
come in different sizes, colours, flavours and textures, and
are sold in packs of about 10 to about 40. You can try a
mixed box to see what size, texture, colours and flavours
you and your partner like. Anyone can buy condoms –
there is no age limit or proof of age required.

Male condoms are 98 per cent effective at preventing
pregnancy 'in an ideal world', meaning when they are
used 'correctly'. In real life this percentage
drops to just under 90 per cent because of
breakage, slippage, not putting them on
well or taking them off at the wrong time
and in the wrong way. When it comes
to preventing STIs, male condoms are
a standout. (See Sexually transmitted
infections on page 243.)

MORE
ON
p. 228

I was in a Christian youth group until I was 16. I realised
when I was 17 that the Pope (John Paul II) didn't
approve of condoms and I said, 'This isn't going
to work for me,' and I quit. *Rocío Marte, 40*

Most male condoms are made from latex, which a small percentage of people have an allergy to. Mostly this causes skin rashes, but in severe cases it could lead to anaphylaxis (a severe, life-threatening allergic reaction). Fortunately, there are alternatives to latex condoms that don't cause allergic reactions. Condoms made from polyurethane don't cause allergies and are also relatively easy to find in shops or online.

Lubricant, aka 'lube'

Many male condoms are pre-lubricated, meaning lubricant was applied before they were packaged. When you take one out of its packet and roll it onto a penis, you'll notice that it feels slightly slippery. For some people this is sufficient lubrication, but you can add extra – just use water-based or silicone-based lube to protect the latex.

WHAT IS LUBRICANT OR 'LUBE'?

This is clear liquid or jelly-like stuff that you buy from the supermarket, convenience store or chemist and use on your genital area to make sexual touching, rubbing etc more slippery and comfortable. Water-based lubricant is the most common because it's safe to use with condoms, but you can also get silicone-based or oil-based (oil-based lube can damage the latex in condoms). In Australia there are national standards that personal lubricant needs to meet to receive approval.

How to be a male condom boss

In my work I teach young people about sexual health and condoms. I encourage young people to try (using) a condom before they need it for sex. They also need to know how to access condoms, and about lube. Some young people think lube goes on BEFORE the condom! (It doesn't!)
Christian, father of two teens

ATTENTION ALL PENIS-OWNERS: if you plan on having oral sex or intercourse with another person at some time in your life, become a condom expert!

PUTTING A CONDOM ON

☆ Male condoms come in individually wrapped packets. Always check the expiry date that's stamped on it – if it's out of date, it's more likely to break. Toss those ones out.

☆ Open the packet carefully – you don't want to tear the condom with teeth or sharp fingernails.

225

☆ The condom will be rolled up and look like a round disc with a 'bubble' in the middle. That bubble is called the 'tip' and is designed to catch semen when you ejaculate while wearing the condom.

☆ Position the condom on the tip of the fully erect penis. If the penis isn't fully erect, wait a bit until it gets there!

☆ Gently squeeze or hold the condom tip between the thumb and finger of one hand so there's no air inside it. (If there's air in the condom tip, there's a greater risk of the condom breaking after you ejaculate inside it because the air and the semen could overstretch it.) With the other hand, roll the entire condom down over the entire penis.

☆ Put a bit of water-based lubricant on the *outside of the condom* if you or your partner want to. It's up to you for penis-in-vagina sex, but we recommend using lube for anal sex.

☆ When you've finished having sex, hold on to the bottom of the condom so it does not slip off the penis while you're pulling out of the vagina or anus. Having it slip off during removal and leak semen is a common 'accident' that can increase the risk of pregnancy or STIs. Semen can also leak if you leave the penis inside the vagina/anal canal after ejaculation and wait too long to pull out – once the erection goes down, semen can leak outside the condom if you leave your penis inside.

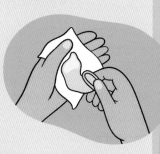

☆ Once your penis is completely outside of the other person's body, gently pull the condom off. Then dispose of your condom properly – tie a knot in the end of it to stop semen spilling out, wrap it up in a tissue and pop it in a bin.

Don't flush condoms (used or unused) down the toilet!

227

My friend almost had sex but the condom came off as it was almost 'there', he ejaculated on her near 'there' and now she is stressing about being pregnant ... What is the chance of this?

Don't panic. Condoms can tear, break or slip off. It can happen when they're not put on properly or the air hasn't been squeezed out of the tip before they're put on. If semen spills inside the vagina, there is a risk of pregnancy – those wriggly sperm are fast swimmers! If the semen spills outside the vagina, such as onto the vulva, or thigh, it's a much lower risk – sperm need the moist environment of the vagina to find their way towards an egg. If pregnancy is a risk, the emergency pill is available over the counter at a pharmacy.

MORE ON p. 239

To give your trusty condom the best chance of NOT breaking:

- Keep condoms in a cool, dry place out of direct sun.
- Check the use-by date.
- Use a new condom each time you have penis-in-vagina sex or anal sex – they're not designed for reuse!
- Leave the condom on the whole time your penis is inside your partner's vagina/anal canal.
- Put it on and take it off correctly.
- If you're using latex condoms, only use a water-based or silicone-based lubricant (not an oil-based one, which can damage the condom).

What does sex feel like with a condom on?

Sex with a condom on can feel different to the same person (or couple) from one time to the next. Many young people equate wearing a condom with having intercourse and it automatically turns them on and makes them feel good. They might also say that it takes away anxiety associated with intercourse because condoms reduce the risk of STIs or pregnancy – the thought of which can be a mood-killer.

Some penis-owners notice that wearing a condom changes the sensitivity of the skin sometimes, but not always. This usually means the intense tingly feeling is dampened down a bit, which is seen as a negative by some people. Others prefer the reduced sensation because it can make an erection and intercourse last longer.

People with a vagina who have penis-in-vagina sex might also find that it feels different when their partner wears a condom. Sometimes one or both people notice that the natural lubrication in the vagina 'dries up', and might find it helpful to use some water-based lube as well.

Female condoms

This is a soft tube, closed at one end, that goes inside the vagina before having penis-in-vagina sex. Female condoms are made from soft plastic. Think of them as a snuggly plastic sock that fits inside and lines the whole inside of the vagina – they cover the cervix and top of the vagina and the sides, right to the vaginal opening. When a penis or other object goes inside, the female condom is a thin barrier that will stop semen, sperm or STIs from getting in.

Female condoms come individually wrapped, like male condoms. To use one, check the expiry date and open the packet. Hold the closed end (which has a thicker ring), squeeze the sides of the flexible inner ring and put it into the vagina. Then use a finger to push the inner ring as high up as it will go (the same way you might push a tampon up). The thin, outer ring of the female condom sits outside the opening of the vagina. To take it out, gently twist the outer ring and pull it out. Throw it in a bin (don't flush it!).

Dental dams

These are thin squares made of the same stuff as male
and female condoms – most are made of latex, but some
are polyurethane.

Dental dams are NOT a contraceptive. They are placed
over the vulva or anal area during oral sex. Dental dams
help stop the spread of STI-causing viruses or bacteria
from the mouth to the genital area, and vice versa. For
example, common cold sores are caused by a virus that
can in turn cause an infection called genital herpes if it
gets onto the genital skin. Dental dams
are sold in pharmacies or online.
Some people make their own dental
dams by repurposing an unused
male condom.

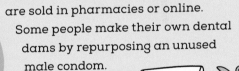

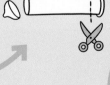

231

The condom conversation

For plenty of teens who want to have (penis-in-vagina or anal) sex, using a condom is a no-brainer. Others need a conversation – which can be mildly awkward to very tricky. Some think that insisting on their partner using a condom is a sign of mistrust or a lack of love. Others say that showing care for each other's health is a sure sign of trust and love!

> I feel like the standard should be *assuming* I'll be using a condom. I'll always bring up condoms. If we're gonna have sex I'll just be like, 'Hey, I'm just gonna go grab a condom.' I feel like if I ask. 'Shall I get a condom?' it sounds like I want it to be optional. *Seb. 19*

Common STIs mostly don't show any symptoms (see Sexually transmitted infections on page 243). This can mean that one person might be carrying an STI from ages ago and unknowingly pass it on to a new partner. That's why using condoms makes such good sense – they stop the spread of STIs.

Remember, it's your body and you get to say what you do and don't want. If you want to use a condom and your partner doesn't, then ask them again. And if they still refuse, you can refuse to have sex with them. It's your choice!

> He didn't know or understand the risks. So I listed some of the diseases he could get. He said, 'What do you mean? I have sex with girls all the TIME and girls NEVER ask me to put on a condom.' *Rocio Marte. 40*

HERE ARE SOME TIPS FOR HAVING THE CONDOM CONVERSATION:

★ Do it before you even start making out – don't wait until 'the heat of the moment'!

☆ Talk about why you do/don't want to use a condom.

★ Don't be afraid to have plentiful supplies of condoms – for you and your friends. Doing so means you're prepared and care about your sexual health and others.

HOW TO ASK FOR/INSIST ON A CONDOM:

★ 'I love condoms, because then I don't have to worry.'

☆ 'I want us to use condoms because if I don't, evil clowns start crawling out of the TV.'

★ 'Who's going to get the condoms this time – you, me, both of us?'

☆ 'I'm not on any other forms of birth control, so it's gotta be condoms!'

★ 'I like to be safe, and I want you to be safe too.'

☆ 'It's my non-negotiable! If you don't want to wear a condom … we can watch e-sports?'

★ 'I know I can relax and enjoy it with a condom. Without it I'm gonna spend the whole time stressing.'

The condom conversation can change over time. If you and your partner are having sex exclusively, and you have been checked for STIs, and you are using other contraception (if pregnancy is a risk), you might decide to give condoms a rest for a while. Or not.

> My mum used to buy 40-packs of condoms ALL THE TIME. She'd leave them in my room and make sure my friends knew they were allowed to grab a handful any time. I became known for always having an available supply. *Anouk, 20*

QUESTIONS FOR DR MELISSA

❝ If you have sex without a condom but the guy takes his penis out of the vagina before he ejaculates, can the girl still get pregnant? ❞

Withdrawal (aka pulling out) is when the penis-owner pulls their penis out of the vagina before they ejaculate. The logic is, no semen gets squirted into the vagina so the sperm can't reach an egg. (Instead, it ends up somewhere outside the vagina – maybe on a thigh, tummy, mattress, floor ...) This sounds OK in theory but is the **least effective method of birth control** for a bunch of reasons.

First, those tricky sperm might sneak into what's called 'pre-cum' – it's the clear fluid that sometimes comes out of a penis during sexual arousal, but before ejaculation. Second, withdrawing one's penis just before ejaculation involves precision timing and control. And that's not always possible! It's estimated that one in five couples who only use the withdrawal method for a year will get pregnant.

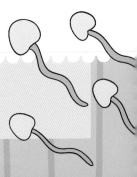

Hormonal contraception

Hormonal contraception is a bunch of different pills, liquids or 'devices' that release hormones into the body of a person with ovaries, a uterus and vagina. They work on different parts of the pregnancy chain.

The hormones contained in these different methods are types of oestrogen and a type of progesterone. Oestrogen and progesterone are made naturally by our bodies. One of their major jobs is to create the menstrual cycle, which also involves ripening and releasing eggs **(aka ovulation)**. In the hormonal methods of contraception, these hormones are 'synthetic', meaning they are made in a laboratory rather than by the body.

'THE PILL' is one of the oldest hormonal contraceptive methods – it's been around for more than 70 years. It contains a type of oestrogen and a type of progesterone, so it's sometimes called the 'combined pill'. It has to be taken every day. It works by stopping an egg from being released with each menstrual cycle: no egg = no pregnancy. It's anywhere from 91 to 99 per cent effective, depending on whether it's taken every day and whether or not it's absorbed properly into the body (vomiting or diarrhoea, for instance, could stop it from getting into the bloodstream).

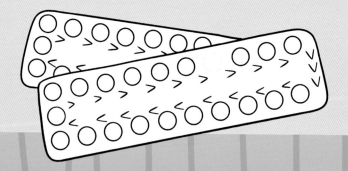

'THE ROD' is a tiny plastic rod about the length of a match (4 cm) and only 2 mm in diameter. Inside the rod is three years' worth of progesterone hormone, which is released very slowly and stops an egg from being released with the menstrual cycle. The rod has to be put into the body – it sits just underneath the skin in the upper arm. It's a very quick and simple procedure that a doctor or nurse can do (for example, in a GP practice or family planning clinic). Effectiveness-wise, the rod wins – it is 99.9 per cent likely to prevent a pregnancy.

THE HORMONE INTRA-UTERINE DEVICE (IUD) is a small, T-shaped plastic gadget that contains progesterone hormone. It works by stopping sperm from getting inside an egg, meaning that fertilisation can't happen. It also thins the lining of the uterus, which means that if an egg does get fertilised, it cannot implant itself in the uterus. It also makes it difficult for sperm to get through to the uterus by thickening the mucus around the cervix. Effectiveness-wise, it's up there with the rod – about 99.8 per cent.

THE 'MINI PILL'

is a tablet that contains only a progesterone hormone, hence the name 'mini'. It works by making the naturally occurring mucus in the cervix too thick for sperm to get through. Occasionally, it can stop ovulation. It's less effective than the rod or the hormone IUD and is also a bit trickier than the Pill because it must be taken at the exact same time every day to work properly.

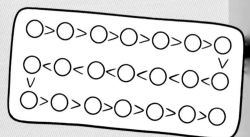

There's a new pill that only contains progesterone hormone. It works like the combined pill, by stopping ovulation. It's more forgiving than the 'mini pill' too; you just need to take it daily, but not at exactly the same hour every day.

THE INJECTION

is a liquid containing a progesterone hormone that is injected (usually) into your butt muscle, and it works by stopping ovulation. Effectiveness is as high as 99.8 per cent, but it only lasts three months. After that, you need another shot.

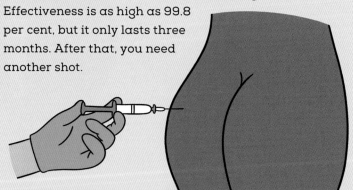

THE VAGINAL RING is made from soft plastic and contains oestrogen and progesterone hormones. You put the ring high up inside the vagina and it releases the hormones through the walls of the vagina. It stays inside the vagina for three weeks, then you take it out for one week if you want to have a period. Then it's time for a new ring. It works by stopping ovulation and is up to 99.5 per cent effective.

THE EMERGENCY PILL used to be called the 'morning-after pill'. It's the contraceptive you may need to take after sex, usually because – oops! – the condom broke, or slipped off, or you missed a few days of the contraceptive pill ... well, sometimes it just happens. If you're worried about the risk of pregnancy, the emergency pill can be taken three to five days after unprotected sex (depending on the emergency pill). It prevents or delays ovulation. On average, the emergency pill is 85 per cent effective, but it's more effective the sooner it's taken after having unprotected penis-in-vagina sex.

This one does not need a doctor's prescription – you can rock up to a pharmacy (on your own if you want to) and buy it over the counter.

Side effects and other important things to know

The good news about hormonal contraception is that it's almost always very safe to use, especially when you're young. Most of the types of hormonal contraception can also help with period pain and heavy periods, and some are good for acne, too. But they can all have side effects (most of which are mild or go away). Get personalised, specific advice from your doctor about what to expect, what happens to your periods when you're on hormonal contraception, and any other questions you have. Ask as often as you need to! If you're after the emergency pill, the pharmacist will explain any side effects and will answer your questions. (See Going to the doctor on page 246.)

Fertility awareness

This method is about avoiding penis-in-vagina sex around the time that the vagina-owner is ovulating. If sperm aren't anywhere near an egg during that time, then the chances of pregnancy are much lower. This method is unpredictable  and unreliable for many people, and has much lower effectiveness rates. But it can be better than nothing! To use this method, you need to know your menstrual cycle very well. This could involve using a period tracker app for a few months, taking your temperature and paying attention to the mucus/discharge in your vagina every day. Putting all this info together, you can come up with a general idea of when you're ovulating. Then, you avoid penis-in-vagina sex for seven days BEFORE you expect ovulation and up until at least 24 hours after.

Copper IUDs

This is a small plastic T-shaped device with copper wire wrapped around it. It is put inside the uterus by a doctor or a nurse and can sit there for five or 10 years (depending on the type). A very thin nylon thread is attached and hangs down into the vagina (which usually cannot be felt) so that the IUD can be removed again later. The copper IUD releases tiny amounts of copper into the body and prevents pregnancy by slowing or stopping the egg and sperm from meeting. It also stops a fertilised egg from being able to implant in the uterus. These are 99.5 per cent effective.

Permanent methods

A permanent method means doing some minor surgery to block off the channels in the body that carry either eggs or sperm. They are over 99 per cent effective. For people with ovaries and a uterus, the Fallopian tubes are blocked using either a metal clip or something called a micro-insert. For people with testicles, the tubes that carry sperm (vas deferens) are cut or blocked. The procedure is called a vasectomy. People under 18 years old are not able to have one of these permanent methods of contraception without going through a legal process in the court. This is because they're considered invasive and irreversible.

Sexually transmitted infections (aka STIs)

" Do you have to use protection during oral sex? I've heard you have to, but how can you give a guy oral sex when he has a condom on? **"**

Sexually transmitted infections are passed from one person to another through sexual contact. So, unlike some other infections, you can't pass them on by coughing, sneezing or shaking hands with someone! If you have an STI, you might pass it on to someone by having penis-in-vagina sex, anal sex or, for some STIs, oral sex.

There are lots of different viruses, bacteria and other microscopic germs that are transmitted through sexual contact. Many of them have no symptoms, so one person might transmit an STI to another person without knowing they have it. Some of them cause serious illness, others less so. Sometimes one particular STI becomes really common and causes a pandemic – this happened in the 1980s with the virus called HIV (Human Immunodeficiency Virus). These days, HIV can be treated with medicine, so people no longer die from it. Medicine can also be taken to prevent it (using a condom also stops it from being spread).

Around the world, HPV (Human Papillomavirus) is the most common STI. Many countries, including Australia, have been giving the HPV vaccine to young teens, which has drastically reduced its spread. HPV can cause cervical cancer, so the vaccine has meant there's been a huge drop in this.

The most common STI today in young people is chlamydia. Another one that's less common, but still getting around, is gonorrhoea. An STI called syphilis used to be really common and still occasionally pops up. All of these are passed on by unprotected penis-in-vagina sex, anal sex or, in some cases, oral sex. Condoms will stop these STIs being passed on. These STIs are easy to test for and easy to cure. You might get tested as a routine part of your self-care, or because you're with a new partner.

Or you might get tested because you have symptoms, such as discharge; painful peeing; pain in your pelvic area or genital parts when you have intercourse; lumps, bumps or something that you're not sure about on your genitals; or itchy genitals.

There's heaps of excellent information out there about STIs, how to look for them and how to get rid of them. Talking to your doctor about getting an STI check is a great way to look after yourself and take control of your sexual health. Sometimes STI education is the only sex ed that teens get in school. And even though that's not NEARLY enough sex ed, it actually is worth knowing about!

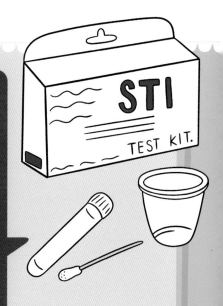

The other day my friends and I, more just for a laugh, went and got STI tests! And I would've been really scared to do that when I was 16! It was a walk-in clinic. I thought it would be a pelvic exam. They gave you these swabs, kind of like a COVID test, and you could just go into the bathroom and do it by yourself. And then I had a really good talk with the doctor about sexual health and sexual wellbeing. Not invasive at all and a really positive experience! *Izzy, 19*

Going to the doctor

Going to the doctor for a bad case of the flu, or a sprained ankle, is one thing. Going to the doctor to talk about sexual health is next level, right?! Well, it doesn't have to be. There are hundreds of doctors out there – Dr Melissa is one of them – who talk to teens and young people about sex and sexual health. It's confidential. It's non-judgemental. It can be really hard to tell a doctor about something as personal and private as sex. But it's worth doing!

Most teens rely on a parent or carer to make a doctor's appointment, take them there and help them get prescriptions filled. But when you're ready to take care of your sexual health, you might want some privacy. If you're comfortable talking to your folks about it, great – research shows this is really good for overall sexual health. If that's a *nuh-uh, no thanks*, you have the right to see a doctor confidentially. Doctors must, by law, keep information confidential unless you are at immediate risk of death or severe harm, or if someone is abusing you.

Over the years I've seen teens in my doctor's office who have had all kinds of needs when it comes to confidentiality. It might be a teen wanting contraception who has brought her mum with her for support because they've already talked about it together and are on the same page! It might be a teen who does not want her parents to know she's having sex with her boyfriend and is seeking out her own care – go her, this takes maturity and courage. It might be a gay teen wanting an STI check who is really scared of his family finding out he's gay. I want him to know that our clinic is welcoming of everybody, and that we can also help him find other support if he wants it. It could be a teen who's worried about erection problems, or porn addiction. *Dr Melissa*

A sexual health visit to a doctor doesn't have to be about STI tests or contraception. Doctors can talk to you about your worries about bodies, genitals, how sex works for your body, sexuality, gender, anxiety, mental health … anything! Your doctor might also be able to help you bring a parent or carer into the conversation if that's what you want.

You can go to the family doctor you've known forever – and you can level up that relationship so they can see you on your own if you want, only sharing information with your carers if you say so. Or you might want a whole new doctor – one close to school or work, who's affordable, or who has been recommended by a friend. (See More resources on page 294 for more information about health services.)

PREGNANCY LOWDOWN

If pregnancy happens when you're a teen, it might be a surprise, a shock, something wanted, or something definitely unwanted. It's common to feel freaked out. There's plenty of help, advice and support out there for pregnant teens. Most importantly, you have the right to make your own decisions. Sometimes it can take a while to know what you want or need.

How do I know if I'm pregnant?

Sometimes the earliest clue that you're pregnant is that your period is late, doesn't come or is unusual (e.g. super-light). Other early symptoms might be tiredness, breast soreness, cramps in your pelvic area, suddenly hating the smell of coffee, or nausea. Even with all the signs, the best way to be sure of pregnancy is to do a pregnancy test. The pregnancy tests that you can buy in the supermarket or chemist are very accurate.

PREGNANT

NOT PREGNANT

If you do a test too early, though, the test might show up negative, so it's important to test a couple of weeks after having unprotected penis-in-vagina sex. If you prefer, you can visit a doctor, who can do the test in their office or order a blood test.

Pregnancy options

With a surprise pregnancy, it can be incredibly tricky figuring out what you want. Getting all the information you need and talking things through with someone can really help. This is a time when you may need to lean on a friend, mother, parent or parent figure for help. That could be an adult like a parent or carer, or it might be a doctor or counsellor.

A pregnant person can choose to terminate or to continue with the pregnancy. It's legal and safe in Australia to get a termination, also called an abortion. (More on the next page.)

If a person chooses to continue, there's a bunch of tests, check-ups and support to help them have a healthy pregnancy and safe birth. They may choose to keep the baby, or the baby can be adopted by another family to raise.

It is ultimately the pregnant person's choice what to do, and they should not feel pressured by friends, family or their partner about what to do next.

Abortion

When choosing to terminate the pregnancy, there's a choice of medical or surgical abortion. A medical abortion is taking pills, 36 to 48 hours apart, which leads to cramping and bleeding, like a heavy period. These pills need to be taken **before nine weeks of pregnancy** (which is counted as nine weeks from your last period). Medical abortion is available via telehealth consultation if you live in a remote area or can't get to a doctor and the pills can be posted out to you. Timing is important here, because this method of abortion is only available **early** in the pregnancy.

A surgical abortion can be a fairly accessible option for people who live in large cities in Australia. Depending on the state or territory, you can get a surgical abortion up to 22 or more weeks. It involves a minor procedure in a clinic with a mild anaesthetic. The type of procedure depends on how many weeks the pregnancy is.

What's a miscarriage?

A miscarriage is when a pregnancy ends by itself. Up to one in five pregnancies end this way, and it usually shows up as heavy bleeding or pain, or both. It often means there is something wrong with the chromosomes of the embryo that meant it couldn't survive – so it's the body's natural way of removing it. Heavy smoking, alcohol, caffeine and some medical conditions might increase the chances of miscarriage, too. There's research happening now that looks at vaping and miscarriage: watch this space.

WHEN PEOPLE HAVE BABIES WITH MEDICAL ASSISTANCE

Penis-in-vagina sex is the way most pregnancies happen, but about 5 per cent of babies in Australia are conceived with medical assistance. It might involve a same-sex couple, or a single person wanting a baby on their own, or a couple having trouble conceiving through penis-in-vagina sex.

Young people who have medical treatments that might affect their ability to conceive later in life can also receive information and advice about medical assistance. This might include children and teens having cancer treatment, or teens having gender-affirming hormones.

You can't get pregnant if you have sex on your period

An egg is usually released by the ovary (aka ovulation) around the middle of the menstrual cycle (usually midway between periods). That's when you're most likely to fall pregnant if you're having unprotected penis-vagina-sex. But it's not a reliable form of contraception to only have sex on your period – in fact, using this method fails about 25 per cent of the time. This is because:

A Menstrual cycles vary in length, especially in teens.

B Sperm can live for up to five days. So even if a person is still bleeding when they have sex, the sperm could survive until ovulation day in some situations.

C Sometimes ovulation happens randomly, a few days earlier than usual.

You can't get a sexually transmitted infection (STI) if you're on the Pill

The Pill is an AMAZING contraceptive, but its superpowers don't extend to stopping those sneaky viruses, bacteria or other tiny organisms from getting into your body. The same is true for other hormonal contraceptives – if you want to prevent STIs, use condoms or dental dams (depending on the type of sex you're having). Lots of heterosexual couples choose to use condoms (which WILL protect you from *most* STIs) AND a hormone contraceptive.

You can't get an STI from anal sex

A lot of the germs that cause STIs love the dark, moist places either around the genital area (which includes the anus) or further inside the reproductive organs and inside the anus. STIs such as chlamydia, gonorrhoea, herpes, HPV, syphilis and HIV can all be passed on through anal sex. Condoms are excellent protection if you're into anal sex and don't want an STI.

AWKWARD SEX MOMENTS AND OTHER CHALLENGES

I heard my parents having sex ... ewww

ADULTS ONLY

> Young people don't want to think of the adults in their lives as sexual, which is funny because adults don't want to see young people as sexual either ... like ... everyone's just awkward about it!
> *Georgia Carr, sex ed researcher*

You might be very comfortable seeing your parents doing adult things like their job, driving a car (especially if it's taking you somewhere you need to go), showing each other affection and joking around together in the kitchen. But sex ... NO THANKS! I'D RATHER EAT A BURGER MADE FROM WORMS. You're naturally programmed to want some space from them, especially about private or personal things like sex. It's also because society in general has a lot of hang-ups about sex. We see it everywhere, but we don't want to talk about it – especially not with parents or other adults!

Sitting with that slightly yuck-feeling and asking yourself why you feel like that can help you think about sex in a different way, like – actually, why *wouldn't* my parents have sex? What's the big deal? If their sex life is distracting – maybe they're a bit noisy, or leave the door open thinking you're asleep – you might want to drop them a hint, or have a conversation with them. (See How do I talk to my parents about sex? on page 26.)

Fanny farts

Fanny farts – also called 'queefing' – are another sign of the vagina's many skills and talents, including its incredible sound effects. The vagina is a stretchy tube that can allow air into it and then back out again. Air gets in from exercises and stretching, or from things going in and out of the vagina – like a finger or a penis. When a penis or some other object moves around inside a vagina, it can push air in, where it gets 'trapped'. The air will find its way out again – sometimes quietly, and other times with a ginormous fart-like sound.

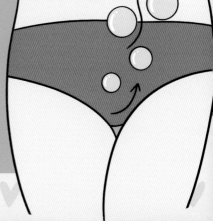

(BTW: A fanny fart is totally different to farts that come from your butt. Those farts happen because digestion of food makes gas inside your intestines.)

Leaks and spills

> I was on top, riding this guy and it was a casual thing, and I leaked a LOT. There was SO MUCH fluid that his belly button overflowed with my juices. *Gemma*

Sex can be a messy business. Gloriously funny, squishy and gooey. When you're turned on, whether on your own or with someone else, juices start to flow as blood gets pumped towards the pelvis and genitals. Vaginal fluid, semen, period flow ... it can all become part of the mix.

Sometimes urine also leaks out during sex or during an orgasm, mostly from people who have a vagina. During intercourse there is pressure close to the bladder and urethra (where pee comes out), and although the pelvic muscles usually stop urine leakage, it can sometimes happen. It doesn't happen much to people with penises because there is a tight ring of muscle between the bladder and urethra that shuts off leakage when the penis is erect. Leaks and spills are a normal part of sex and pleasure.

Sex on your period

It's absolutely OK to have sex when you're on your period if you want to! Being on your period is NOT a protection against pregnancy if you're having penis-in-vagina sex and not using contraception. If the sex you want to have doesn't involve anything going into your vagina, then you can leave your tampon or cup in. If the sex you want to have involves something going IN your vagina, then you'll need to remove your tampon or menstrual cup first. And it'll be a little messier, cos there's menstrual blood and flow still coming out, so you might want to have a towel underneath you. Your partner might want a towel to wipe their hand/face/penis afterwards too.

My parents won't let me have sex

> **My boyfriend and I are so in love, I feel as if we could be together forever, but my parents won't let me see him because when he was over at my house he fingered me and licked me out. I'm 13 and my parents think that I am too young for a sexual relationship.**

You've probably noticed now that you're in your teens that your parents allow you to do some of the more grown-up things while putting the brakes on others. It's a tricky time for everyone! Parents want their kids to be happy and safe – and that's no different when it comes to sex and relationships. But it's not uncommon for teens to feel like their parents don't understand, and sometimes there are real clashes between parents' and teens' beliefs about sex. Every family will have its own rules and ways of negotiating them, but it all starts with communication.

Figure out what you want your parents to know and what you want to ask of them. Find a time to get their full attention and ask them to explain their point of view. Sex is a mature thing to be doing – and so is having a decent conversation with your parents.

MORE ON p. 26

What age is appropriate for a sleepover (with sex)?

I find it interesting that kids as young as 15 are being allowed sleepovers with their teen partner – I would not allow this, but other parents do. Parents' rules are important, and it's good to have these conversations with our kids. *Brenda, parent of two teens*

Figuring out when it's OK to have a partner sleep over in your bed with you is another negotiation between parents and their teens. Those conversations can continue way beyond high school, too – not every family has the space in their house to have partners staying over regularly. Figuring out how to talk with your parents about your wishes and their rules is part of living together.

IS SOMETHING WRONG?

Painful sex

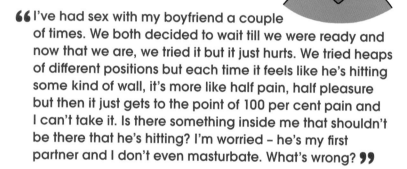

QUESTIONS FOR DR MELISSA

❝ I've had sex with my boyfriend a couple of times. We both decided to wait till we were ready and now that we are, we tried it but it just hurts. We tried heaps of different positions but each time it feels like he's hitting some kind of wall, it's more like half pain, half pleasure but then it just gets to the point of 100 per cent pain and I can't take it. Is there something inside me that shouldn't be there that he's hitting? I'm worried – he's my first partner and I don't even masturbate. What's wrong? ❞

❝ Whenever I have sex it is really painful when the penis first goes in! What does this mean? ❞

❝ I'm a 15-year-old girl, I've been fingered a couple of times. Every time, it hurts. I have never tried using a tampon cos I'm scared it would hurt. Is this normal and would I be able to have (penis-in-vagina) sex without being in a lot of pain??? ALSO my boyfriend now has asked me to have sex! But I'm too scared it will hurt way too much. WILL I BE OK? ❞

260

Sex should NOT be painful, so if it is – STOP the sex you're having!

Plenty of teens worry about painful sex because they've either heard about it or experienced it. That fear can grow from the first time they used a tampon and it felt a bit … *yowch*. Perhaps it hurt from fingering? If that's been the case, it makes sense that the thought of a penis going inside their vagina is quite alarming. But hang on a sec! The incredible teen vagina is stretchy and naturally moist. It's also smart. It has its own strong wall of muscle and supportive pelvic floor muscles that will tighten up like a reflex if it thinks something coming near it will hurt.

'Vaginismus' describes this sort of contraction. Doctors and sex therapists use the word vaginismus when the vagina and pelvic muscles repeatedly spasm and hurt, either when something touches the opening of the vagina OR spasms occur with just the thought of it happening. Don't rush to self-diagnose with vaginismus if you're still getting the hang of sex and want to take your time exploring what's pleasurable, though – you may just need to be more aroused, and therefore lubricated, for sex to be painless.

The body, and particularly the vagina, wants and needs to be turned on before it lets anything go inside it during sex. If you have a vagina, then learning what feels good on your own really can help prep you for when you let another person go near it.

If you'd like to have sex with someone with a vagina, check in with what feels pleasurable for them. Arousal will turn on the vagina's natural lubrication system even if nothing actually goes near it. Sometimes it's best to put penis-in-vagina sex on hold until you've both had time to explore – it can be more pleasurable, exciting and fun to slow things down.

Sometimes painful sex is because of the angle of the penis or sex toy – it can feel like a painful stab near your guts. Experience, asking and readjusting can fix this.

Sometimes pain is felt deeper inside – not at the opening of the vagina. This can happen with an infection high up in the vagina, or the cervix or pelvis, or with some conditions such as endometriosis.

ENDOMETRIOSIS IS A COMMON CONDITION WHERE THE TISSUE THAT LINES THE UTERUS ALSO GROWS OUTSIDE THE UTERUS, SUCH AS IN THE TUBES OR LINING AROUND THE PELVIC AREA. IT AFFECTS FIVE TO 10 PER CENT OF TEENAGERS AND YOUNG WOMEN. THE MOST COMMON SYMPTOM IS PAIN – IT CAN COME AT ANY TIME, AND IS NOT RELATED SPECIFICALLY TO SEX.

Another type of pain is outside, in the vulva. There is a condition called vulvodynia where a vulva-owner might feel a burning sensation near the opening of the vagina. Sometimes it's in a different part of the vulva, up near the clitoris. It isn't always related to sex – the pain can be felt at other times.

Anything that is painful in the genital area – whether it's related to sex or not – deserves to be checked by a doctor. Remember, this is supposed to be a pleasure zone. And even if you're not looking for pleasure or sex, don't put up with pain. Yep, it's awkward presenting to the doctor with a problem with your genitals, but this is part of the practice and learning that gets you off your L-plates. Sorry!

Premature ejaculation

> How long do most guys last, 'cause my bf doesn't last very long during sex and I think he gets embarrassed when he's finished before I do (or before I even get started). How can we both overcome this problem??? Please help us, our sex life is killing our relationship. "

Premature ejaculation is when you ejaculate earlier than you want to. It's one of the most common sex worries that young people have. It's a bit like learning about braking and accelerating when you're driving a car. It takes time to learn control – and in the meantime, it can be stressful and embarrassing!

Often, premature ejaculation is related to anxiety. It might be general anxiety in life or, more specifically, anxiety about

sex. A lot of young men feel pressure to 'perform' during sex, and feel pressure to know exactly what they're supposed to do. It can also be caused by over-excitement – you're just SO horny and turned on that you explode!

If premature ejaculation happens once, it can make you more anxious the next time, and the next time ... till you're caught in a vicious cycle. Experts recommend trying to slow things down **on your own** first. You can do

265

this through masturbating – and taking longer than usual. Stop and start and 'edge' closer to orgasm without actually getting there.

If you're having sex with another person, communicating about **how you want to do things** really helps. It might feel super awkward but if you can both survive the embarrassment

(and you will!), it'll make it WAY better for both of you. Avoid the thing that sets you off too fast, and experience mutual pleasure without jumping straight into intercourse or oral sex.

Some medications have also been found to help people with premature ejaculation. And sometimes counselling for general anxiety helps with sex and relationships, too! You can get advice about these by talking to a doctor or other services for young people (see More resources on page 294.)

Erection problems

66 I've been going out with my bf for about seven months now, and we have been trying to have sex for the past month, except every time we try, he can't get it up for long enough ... I'm starting to think it's me – am I the problem? 99

66 Hi, I am a 19-year-old male. My girlfriend and I recently wanted to have sexual intercourse and nothing rose. What is wrong with me? My girlfriend now thinks I am not attracted to her, but I am. What do I do? Is there any pills or drugs I can take to help me get it up? 99

Penises don't always behave the way we want or expect them to. Teenagers have massive hormone fluctuations, causing wet dreams and unwanted erections in the middle of maths! The other extreme is when it just won't get up.

Problems getting an erection, or keeping it up for the duration of sexual play, are common, even in young people. For those on their sex L-plates, it can be about practising on your own and taking time to figure out what you enjoy. It could be about putting down your phone and trying to masturbate without porn. If you've been conditioned

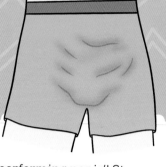

to stay erect while only watching porn, it may feel weird when having sex without porn, and with a real person. Getting used to being present in the moment, with a human body, can start when you're by yourself.

Erection problems in younger people are sometimes simply due to nerves – worrying about what the other person will think, or worrying about 'failure'. Remember the picnic table of options? Try feasting on something that doesn't require an erect penis – you can still enjoy yourselves and it will take the focus off the

'performing penis'! Stress, depression, anxiety, alcohol or other drugs, past trauma, relationship problems – all these things can also affect erections. So can some medical conditions and some medications, so getting an overall health check might be something to consider.

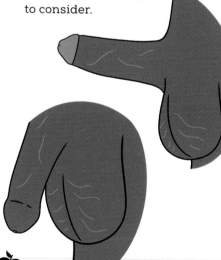

Porn addiction

Researchers aren't sure if addiction to porn is an actual scientific thing the way that drug addiction is. But they do know that watching porn can be a real problem for some people. The best way to decide if you have an addiction to porn is to check in with how it makes you feel. And whether it's interfering with your day-to-day life, including your relationships. Becoming so anxious about when you'll be able to watch porn again that you obsess about it could be a sign. Or doing things like skipping class, not doing homework or seeing friends because you feel a need to watch porn. Preferring to watch porn than do sexy stuff with a real person is another sign.

There's often shame and secrecy tied up with watching porn that makes it difficult to talk about openly, which can make anxiety worse. If you're wondering whether you're 'addicted' to porn you can try to stop or reduce it yourself – that usually works.

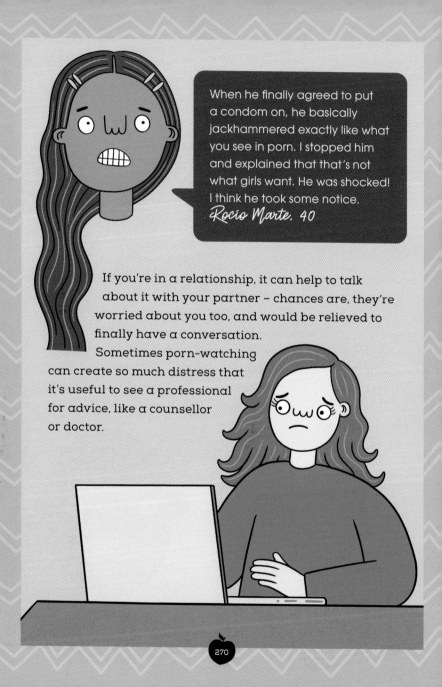

When he finally agreed to put a condom on, he basically jackhammered exactly like what you see in porn. I stopped him and explained that that's not what girls want. He was shocked! I think he took some notice.
Rocio Marte, 40

If you're in a relationship, it can help to talk about it with your partner – chances are, they're worried about you too, and would be relieved to finally have a conversation.

Sometimes porn-watching can create so much distress that it's useful to see a professional for advice, like a counsellor or doctor.

Can't orgasm

66 I'm 18 years old and haven't had an orgasm yet. My boyfriend and I are getting frustrated with it. Is there something wrong with me? We have tried everything. 99

66 My boyfriend and I have had sex about six or seven times now and still I get no pleasure out of it. It's like the whole time I just wait for it to be over. Is there something wrong with me? After sex we usually talk about it and he asks me if it was good and I lie and say yes so he doesn't get hurt. I don't know what to do. 99

Most people have difficulty reaching orgasm at *some* time in their life.

It happens more often when two cisgender, heterosexual people have sex.

Whatever your gender, if you can't orgasm, one thing is certain – it's almost never anything to do with you or your body. The human brain has ways to allow bodies, in all their diversity, to feel sexual pleasure and orgasm. Not being able to orgasm is more likely to do with stress, expectations, communication (or lack of it), and not being able to shake off the images you've seen on TV or porn that make orgasm look as natural and effortless as sneezing.

It's only when I'm with myself that I can get there. Somebody's made me come I think once. Orgasm isn't the main thing for me when I'm having sex. So long as it's enjoyable, it doesn't really matter to me. *Tiger, 19*

I feel huge pressure to orgasm and feel really bad when I can't every time. I can't show him how much I do like this. I know that's not the point, but I do also just want to show it! It's a really good signifier that it's over. *Ramona, 17*

It could be that you don't actually like your partner, or that they're not treating your pleasure as important. But if you don't know how to orgasm by yourself, it's going to be way more tricky to orgasm in partnered sex. (For more on this, check out Getting intimate with myself on page 30 and Orgasms on page 64.) There can be times when a health issue such as depression, anxiety, physical illness or some medications can affect sexual pleasure, including orgasm.

Faking an orgasm is exactly what it sounds like: while having sex with another person, you pretend you're having an orgasm. Research tells us that it's usually women who fake it while having sex with men, not the other way around. This alone should ring alarm bells! When these women were asked why they'd faked it, they'd say things like 'I didn't want to hurt his feelings' or 'I just wanted to get it over with' … which really means 'my pleasure isn't important as long as his ego isn't bruised' OR 'I don't even want to be having sex with him'. It's also saying that orgasm is all that matters. Wrong on many levels!

Do yourself a favour and let yourself feel what you feel, when you feel it – without faking anything. You don't have to orgasm every time you have sex, and just because you do one time doesn't mean you have to EVERY time (or vice versa).

What's the deal with vaginal discharge?

Discharge is one of the last taboos. It's weird that people don't talk about it because, basically, EVERYONE with a vagina experiences vaginal discharge! The fluid is made up of mucus from the cervix and fluid from the vaginal walls. It's a sign that your vagina is a healthy microbiome (aka

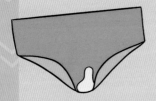

'ecosystem with lots of healthy microorganisms that protect it against germs'). The **average** amount is slightly less than one teaspoon every 24 hours. It leaks out slowly and leaves a small mark on your undies, and it is totally normal!

You might've gone from having none at all when you were a little kid to suddenly seeing it on your undies every day from about 10–12 years old onward. That's also totally normal and a sign that puberty is working its hormonal magic. Discharge is slightly acidic so when it gets on your undies, it can sometimes bleach the colour out of them.

If your discharge suddenly ramps up in volume, has a nasty big smell and is accompanied by a terrible itch, you could have thrush or an STI. Thrush isn't necessarily caused by any sexual activity, and it can be treated with a single trip to the chemist. Go immediately if you think you have it! The longer you wait, the more you'll suffer. An unusually huge amount of discharge is a clear sign something is wrong. There is medicine that will help you, and no-one at the chemist or doctor's will judge you.

Sore or itchy after sex

> **Sometimes when I have sexual intercourse with my boyfriend and we go on for longer than usual, the next day my vagina gets itchy and a bit sore and red, even when I'm going to the toilet. Could this be because of the type of condom we use? Is this dangerous? Please help, I'm worried!**

Just as sex should never be painful, after-sex shouldn't be either. People with all kinds of genitals and bodies might experience a dull throbbing sensation after sex (regardless of whether they used a condom) because the area becomes engorged with blood. It mostly feels pleasant but can be mildly uncomfortable and will go away once the blood flows out again. If there's been a lot of friction during intercourse, both parties could have genitals that feel like sore, overworked muscles. But lasting pain, itchiness or redness that's there the next day is not something you should expect.

Sensitivity or an allergy to the latex in the condom can cause irritation to the lining of the vagina, making it red, swollen, itchy or sore. It will happen each time it's exposed to latex but not if you use a non-latex condom. Painful urination after sex can be a sign of a urinary tract infection (UTI), which is fairly common in people with vaginas (and very rare in people with penises). Symptoms of a UTI are pain, burning or stinging when you pee, and peeing frequently. The urine might also be cloudy or smelly. A visit to your doctor so they can take a urine sample and offer antibiotics will help. Meanwhile, drink plenty of water.

TIPS FOR VAGINA-OWNERS

Peeing straight after sex may help to flush out any bacteria from your urethra, and help you avoid developing a UTI. It won't prevent pregnancy or STIs, though.

condoms
LATEX-FREE

REAL FEEL!

KEEPING SAFE

One of the things that frustrates me is that we have taught teens that 'safe sex' means 'use protection against STIs or pregnancy'. Sure, that knowledge is super important, but feeling safe when it comes to sex is also about so much more. It's about looking after your body, heart, mind and spirit – being able to give and receive consent, about valuing yourself and who you are, and about everybody's rights being respected. *Dr Melissa*

L

'L-plates sex' can feel risky because it's very new. You might not be sure of what to do, you might have nerves ... but deep down, it should feel safe. Safety is something we might be able to control, sometimes, but there's a lot in the world that is *not* within our control.

You'll make some of the trickiest choices in your entire life during your teen years. Adolescence is also when you're most vulnerable.

If staying safe were easy, we'd all be doing it! But it's complex and needs to be approached from multiple angles.

Alcohol

It's a reality that teens drink alcohol before they're legally allowed to buy it. (Your generation didn't invent this, BTW, it's been happening since Santa was a baby!) There's a sensible reason why it's illegal to sell alcohol to people under 18: by reducing its supply, the risk of drunk people coming into serious physical harm or death is also reduced. Alcohol makes many people feel lighter in the head and more relaxed, and also more likely to fall over and hurt themselves and do stupid stuff. It makes human judgement and reaction times worse.

And alcohol plus sex can be a real hot mess.

Here's the deal with **alcohol and sex**: someone who is really drunk cannot give consent. So by getting sloshed, they've become a no-go zone. That's OK, but keep in mind that it goes both ways: if *you're* off your face, you can't give consent. Not true consent. So you may feel like you want to do this thing, but would you *really* want to do it if you were sober?

Even a little alcohol can corrupt judgement in a sexual situation – we might be OK to give consent but be less careful about, say, using a condom. We might be more sloppy and forceful when trying to get someone to have sex with us, and less able to process what they're saying – especially if they're saying no.

When alcohol is messing up consent, dial down your expectations. You thought you'd be shagging in the spare room tonight, but the person you fancy is pretty drunk? Maybe you can flirt and spoon on the couch instead. (It's not actually a worse outcome.) And if you're planning on being too drunk to recite your home address? Maybe you need to have a conversation with yourself and your friends – WHILE SOBER – about where your sex boundaries lie and how'd you like to make sure they're respected.

You don't feel safe

If you're ever in a situation where you're creeped out, you feel unsafe and/or you have the sudden urge to bail – *trust* your gut instincts. It's tempting to tell yourself, 'This can't be happening!' or 'I'm overreacting' – but the feelings of your heart racing, your breathing getting faster, your tummy feeling tense/sick or that horrible scared and panicky feeling are all ways that your body is telling you 'WATCH OUT' or 'GET OUT'.

It could be more subtle than that – any situation where you're feeling the atmosphere change and you don't like it? OK, you're listening to your gut instinct. Now what? As quickly as you can, get into a safe situation. Can you call a friend, move into a public space, call a parent, get a lift?

If you're in a situation where there's no-one to call or ask for help, you need to shore up your personal resources as best you can. Get your clothes on, shoes on, have your keys, phone and money on your body and don't be afraid to run if you have to, or scream. F*** politeness!

Our need to seem cool can sometimes override our gut instinct. Don't worry about how you seem. If it turns out you had nothing to panic about, at least you can laugh at yourself from your position of safety. You can be uncool while you climb into your nice, safe bed.

An unsafe situation could be getting into a car with a driver who seems a bit drunk. It could be finding yourself alone with an adult who's low-key creeping you out. It could be hooking up or going on a date with someone and finding they're seriously hassling you. It's great if you know how to avoid an unsafe situation, but sometimes we simply don't know until it's happening. It's good to chat to adults, such as your parents or carers, about hypothetical situations and talk through strategies for keeping safe.

If you're feeling unsafe online – screenshot what's happening, tell someone, and go offline. If someone says something threatening to you online, tell an adult that you trust. It's *literally* their job to help you.

BANK
0000 0000
00/0

The first sex I had was terrible. I was 18 and he was 28. That age gap – at that age – was too much. I was trying so hard to pretend I was his age and he loved that because it meant he could ignore how scared I was. I was scared. I consented, but it wasn't good. *Anonymous*

Relationship abuse

Relationship abuse means a pattern of behaviour that happens between two people in an intimate relationship, where one person uses verbal or physical threats against the other, or plays mind games with them, or repeatedly pressures them into doing intimate things. The abuser basically tries to control the other person. It can happen to anyone – from celebrities to teens in their first relationships, people in same-sex relationships, to elderly couples.

Signs of relationship abuse:

- Saying things to shame you or make you feel unworthy
- Keeping track of where you are or demanding to know what you're doing all the time
- Posting rude or hurtful things about you on social media or trying to control your social media
- Blaming you if they feel bad or something goes wrong, rather than being able to look objectively at a situation
- Telling you how you should dress or look, or who you should hang out with
- Threatening or actually harming you – physically or sexually

KIERA

WHERE ARE YOU???

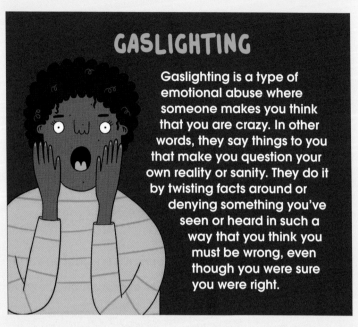

GASLIGHTING

Gaslighting is a type of emotional abuse where someone makes you think that you are crazy. In other words, they say things to you that make you question your own reality or sanity. They do it by twisting facts around or denying something you've seen or heard in such a way that you think you must be wrong, even though you were sure you were right.

If you're in an abusive relationship, you might find you still really love or care for the person who is abusing you. But remember: you matter, and you deserve help. The abuser is also in need of help, but you are not the right person to help them – so a good first step is to take action for yourself, and trust that everyone will be better off.

Talking to your parents or carers is often a great place to start – no-one will love or care for you more than them. If that's not a solution for you, there are confidential helplines, school counsellors and emergency shelters. (See More resources on page 294.)

Getting help

HELP.

Teens often wrote to the magazine column Dolly Doctor asking for help. Sometimes I knew I could help by providing information, like by explaining that feeling horny is common and normal. Other times, I knew that help would need to involve the teen talking to a real person. I got the message that going and asking for help was really scary for them. I also knew that the thought of getting help and taking the first steps were always the hardest part. I know this from seeing thousands of teens in my work as a doctor, too. We wouldn't want to see our loved ones struggling alone, so we shouldn't do it ourselves. *Dr Melissa*

If you're in a situation that's an emergency or crisis, call 999. If you're deaf or have a hearing or speech impairment, you can text 999 to contact the police, fire or ambulance services.

More often, getting help is a process. It's about being able to figure out, with the support of adults, how to recognise danger, stay safe, look after yourself (and your friends) and grow up feeling more confident, healthy and well.

Getting help could be as simple as having a conversation with a parent or carer; sometimes, what seems like an overwhelming situation can be sorted out just like that. Maybe your parent or carer can step in and put an end to a plan that you weren't comfortable with, but felt you couldn't get out of. It could be about your own problem, a friend's problem, or someone you're romantically interested in but not sure about. Talking it through with an adult you trust can help you figure out what you're feeling and thinking.

Sometimes a parent or carer isn't enough, or isn't the right person to seek help from. You might prefer to try another relative, a family friend, or the parent of one of your friends – you'll be able to suss out who feels right. Sometimes the help you need will come from a professional. Fortunately, there is plenty of help out there – but it can be hard to know where to start.

If you already know a professional who you trust, start there. It might be a school counsellor, teacher, your family doctor (GP), a youth counsellor or worker. They might be able to help directly, or help you find the best services for what you need. (See Going to the doctor on page 246 for information about confidentiality and what's involved when you see a professional.)

My friend's boyfriend was really struggling with suicidal thoughts. I said, 'Have you told him to call Lifeline? Or Kids Helpline?' She said, 'Isn't that only for really desperate people?' I said, 'Having suicidal thoughts is enough – he's allowed to call!' *Yumi*

HAVE FUN AND REMEMBER …

The teen years bring a kind of magical discovery to sex – something that is as old as humankind. Wherever that discovery takes you, it's worth celebrating. YOU are worth celebrating.

Make sure you're really ready

If you think you're *not* ready, then *don't do it* … you've got the rest of your life.

If you think you *are* ready, then check:

* Do I know how to care for my body?
* Do I know how to communicate what I like and don't like?
* Do the reasons I'm going to have sex now line up with my values?
* Do I respect myself and the person I'm going to have sex with?

This checklist is the same whether you're a teen or, *ahem* a senior/much-older person.

Once you jump in, you don't have to stay in

Sex with another person is a truly intimate thing, whether they're a long-term partner or someone you barely know. Whatever your reasons for having sex, you might decide you want to stop having sex. That could be in the moment, or after you've had sex a few, or lots of, times. It's totally OK. Just like with driving – you don't have to drive all the time. You might have months, or even years, not getting behind the wheel.

Having sex if and when you choose does not change who you are – it's part of being alive. The same goes for choosing to stop having sex. You're in charge of your body and what you do with it.

Pleasure is key

Everyone equally deserves pleasure if they want it. Sex is, above all, sexy! And pleasurable! So remember:

BE POSITIVE ABOUT SEX. That means feeling safe and having a positive attitude towards pleasure. Pleasure comes from respecting yourself and other people, and from consensual sexual experiences. It comes from embracing the right of all people to be who they are, regardless of gender or sexuality.

Sexual pleasure means being inclusive and celebrating that people, and pleasure experiences, are **diverse**.

TALK SEXY. No, this is not about 'talking dirty'! It's about using language that's respectful, accurate (such as using the correct words for our private parts) and being confident about naming pleasure as an important aspect of sex.

EMBRACE LEARNING. This encourages people to do more research and gain more knowledge about the role of pleasure in sexual health and feeling happy and well.

LOVE YOURSELF. Be kind to yourself.

Know your worth

Sex could be a teeny tiny insignificant part of your world. Or it could be something that matters a LOT. It might be really important to you to figure out your sexual identity and give it a name. Or not. As you move through your teen years learning about sex, there could be plenty of wobbly starts, disappointing endings, wrong turns, U-turns, embarrassing moments, heartache, pure delight and laugh-out-loud fun.

Along the way, not everyone remembers to be kind. Some people are simply afraid of what they don't understand. L-plates sex can be harsher than we'd wish.

That's why knowledge really is power. Not as in 'I want to rule the world' power. But the power of self-knowledge: knowing your body, your pleasure, your feelings, values and who you want to be in the world. That will bring self-respect as you toss around questions about where you fit in, and who's important in your life and why, and realise how much you matter to other people.

> Tell people to just be who they are. I just need to listen to myself. Mum teaches me things over and over, Mum says listen to yourself. Life is not much fun having autism, but it's just who I am. Some teenagers who don't have disabilities are not like that – maybe they argue with their parents, or do other things. I am who I am.
> *Billy, 21, with autism and intellectual disability*

If you are getting a vibe that someone is not treating you with respect, trust your instincts. If it feels safe, communicate your feelings to them. Talk to a trusted adult. We are here to help and support you.

Knowing your worth means self-care. AND allowing others to care for you. It means calling out offensive behaviour, saying 'that's not OK'. It means that in your moments of sex and intimacy with another person, there's genuine acceptance, honesty and kindness.

You've got this. Take good care ... and have fun!

Dr Melissa and Yumi xx

EXPAND YOUR VOCABULARY

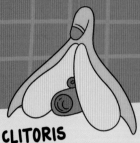

CLITORIS
A highly sensitive part of the body that sits in front of the vagina and has a tip that can be seen near the top of the vulva.

CONSENSUAL
When all people involved in doing something together give consent (aka permission) for it to happen.

ALLY
Someone who is outside a particular community but who stands up for and supports them.

ASEXUAL
Someone who has zero or little sexual attraction to anybody.

CISGENDER
When a person's gender identity is the same as the gender they were presumed to be at birth.

EROGENOUS ZONE

Anywhere on the body that, when touched, turns you on sexually/makes you sexually aroused.

GENDER

A person's sense of being female, male or something else (e.g. non-binary, agender, gender fluid ...).

GENITALS

The outside parts of the body at the lower end of the pelvic area, between the legs, which are highly sensitive and often involved in sexual activities.

HETEROSEXUAL

Someone who is sexually attracted to people of the opposite gender.

HOMOPHOBIA

Being afraid of and/or abusive towards people who are not heterosexual.

HORMONES

Chemicals made by special tissues in the body called glands. Each hormone is a 'messenger' – it is sent through the bloodstream to tell another tissue to do or not to do something. Puberty hormones do lots of special jobs, including getting us turned on sexually.

291

INTERCOURSE

Throughout this book the word 'intercourse' means EITHER penis-in-vagina OR penis-in-anus (anal) sex.

LGBTQIA+

Stands for lesbian, gay, bisexual, trans, queer or questioning, intersex, asexual, plus. It represents diverse people and a huge range of sexuality or gender identities.

MASTURBATION

Touching your own genitals (usually with your hands) for sexual pleasure. (Mutual masturbation can be two people doing this to each other.)

LUBE/LUBRICANT

Something used to reduce friction in sex and make it more comfortable. Lube might be used for penis-in-vagina sex, anal sex, or masturbation/mutual masturbation.

ORAL SEX

Using the mouth, tongue and lips to touch the other person's genitals for sexual pleasure.

ORGASM

A combination of physical and psychological sensations that build up and peak, creating an intense, pleasurable feeling.

SEXUAL AROUSAL

This is a rather *boring* medical expression that basically means getting turned on, feeling horny, excited, randy ... Sexual arousal involves physical and emotional changes in the body such as a faster heart rate and feeling excited. But what makes a person get 'sexually aroused' can change all the time.

PORN

Pictures or videos showing people's genitals or people having sex, with the intention of causing sexual arousal. The people involved are models or actors.

STI

Stands for sexually transmitted infection. A bunch of bacteria, viruses and other kinds of microscopic organisms can be sexually transmitted. This means you can't catch them from, say, coughing on someone, but you can catch them from various kinds of sex.

TRANSPHOBIA

Being afraid of and/or abusive towards people who are not cisgender (e.g. trans, non-binary, agender, gender fluid ...).

MORE RESOURCES

amaze.org

newsexslang.com

scarleteen.com

bishuk.com

sexetc.org

thepleasureproject.org

itstimewetalked.com

WHEN YOU USE THE INTERNET TO FIND OUT ABOUT SEX, IT'S BEST TO STICK WITH **DOT GOV**, **DOT ORG** AND **DOT EDU** SITES TO AVOID ENDING UP ON SITES YOU DON'T WANT TO BE ON.

ACKNOWLEDGEMENTS

This book is dedicated to the tens of thousands of young people who wrote to the Dolly Doctor column over the 46 years of the magazine's life. I had the honour of answering some of your questions in the latter half of that lifetime. I learned so much from your thirst for knowledge about what it is to be sexual in all its diversity. I jointly dedicate this book to the hundreds of young people who continue to share their stories with me – as a doctor, researcher, educator and advocate. You inspire me every day. Thank you to Yumi, Marisa Pintado and Benython Oldfield for your unstinting support, yet again. And to Jenny Latham, without whom this book simply would not be. Your gorgeous illustrations and intuition bring life, meaning and connection to facts and ideas in ways that words alone never could. Thank you to the young people who so generously shared their thoughts, experiences and wisdom with me: Billy, Casper, Dominique, Fatema, Grace, Holly, Jane, Jessie, Lisa, Meghan, Natalie, Sahib and Tom. A huge thank you to Betty Nguyen for reaching out to the Wellbeing, Health and Youth Commission on my behalf and, in doing so, contributing to the richness of young people's voices. And to the parents of teens: Bibi, Brenda, Christian, Geraldine, Nuzhat and Sharon – this book is enriched by your insights. Thank you to the following professionals and colleagues, many of whom I am privileged to call friends, whose deep knowledge fortifies every page in this book: Alan McKee, Amie Hill, Bernard Salibi, Brenda Armstrong, Chantelle Otten, Christopher Fisher, Cristyn Davies, Deborah Bateson, Eva Jackson, Georgia Carr, Jacqueline Hellyer, Jacqui Hendriks, Jenny Walsh, Kath Albury, Katrina Marson, Kerry Robinson, Lauren French, Maree Crabbe, Melanie Wilson, Nina Livingstone, Peter Chown, Rachel Skinner, Renee West, Rudi Bremer and Steph Lum. Thank you to the rest of team Hardie Grant – Pooja Desai, Penny White, Joanna Wong, Luna Soo, Emma Schwarcz, Kristy Lund-White and Amanda Shaw. Big thanks to Tess Walsh-Rossi, Judy Li and Saskia Roberts for your help in sifting through the Dolly Doctor archives. Thank you to Mitchell for being my sounding board and steadfast supporter. To my darling children: Julian, Samantha, Georgia and Hannah – thank you for being part of this book in so many ways, most of all for having many an awkward conversation with me over many years.

Dr Melissa

Thank you to all the people, young and fully adult, who opened their hearts and talked about their experiences of sex for this book. That raw honesty is so beautiful to witness and gives our readers a wonderful insight into the diversity of experiences that make up what's 'normal'. A big thank you to booksellers, teachers and librarians around the world: you really are critical in getting our books into the hands of readers. We love you, we see you, we appreciate you! It's such a cliche to say – but all we want is for our books to end up in the hands of those who need it.

A huge, crying hug of appreciation to the hard-working team at Hardie Grant: Pooja Desai, Penelope White, Joanna Wong, Luna Soo, Emma Schwarcz, Kristy Lund-White and Amanda Shaw. And thank you to my IRL friends who have stepped up and been magnificent in making me feel eruptions of delight and appreciation and who have shown me the wonders of human love, fun, silliness and resilience.

Thanks to the team of amazing creators at ABC's podcast *Ladies, We Need to Talk* – producers, engineers, execs and sound designers past and present, your wonderful hard work informs this work.

Thank you to Benython Oldfield, Claudine Ryan, Marisa Pintado and most of all, the inimitable, legendary Dr Melissa Kang.

Yumi

CONTRIBUTORS

Thank you so much to our wonderful contributors:

Alan McKee, Amie Hill, Angie, Bernard Salibi, Bibi, Billy, Brenda, Cara, Casper, Chantelle Otten, Charlotte, Christian, Dr Christopher Fisher, Claire, Cristyn Davies, Professor Deborah Bateson, Declan, Dominique, Dr Eva Jackson, Fatema, Gemma, Georgia Carr, Geraldine, Grace, Hannah Carr, Holly, Izzy, Jacqueline Hellyer, Dr Jacqui Hendriks, Jane, Jenny Walsh, Jessie, Josh, Julian Carr, Professor Kath Albury, Professor Kerry Robinson, Lauren French, Lisa, Madeleine Stewart, Maree Crabbe, Meghan, Melanie Wilson, Natalie, Nina Livingstone, Nuzhat, Peter Chown, Phoebe, Professor Rachel Skinner, Ramona, Rocío Marte, Rudi Bremer, Sahib, Samantha Carr, Seb, Steph Lum, Tiger, Tom and others who have wished to remain anonymous.

Your honesty is so appreciated.

Jenny Latham is an illustrator from the United Kingdom. Since graduating from Falmouth University in 2019, Jenny has illustrated all four books in the *Welcome to* series. Jenny's biggest passion is making people feel empowered, positive and proud. Jenny has enjoyed every single second she's spent working on this series and feels extremely lucky to illustrate such important topics.